MINDWORKS ART

a spiritual journey

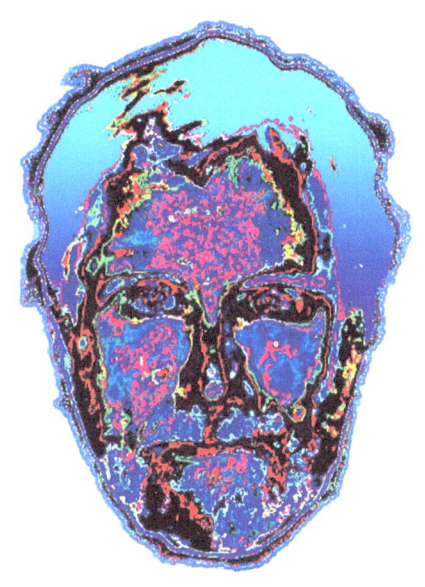

by Richard Fisher

Website: http://www.MINDWORKSart.com
Email: richard@mindworksart.com

Title ID: 3846880
ISBN-13: 978-1503278240

Printed by CreateSpace.com

Front Cover: *Oz Head*

The origin of this image is a photo of my head which was modified with filters in Photoshop program. The Wizard of Oz is a 'humbug', an ego--not a god who originates images but the one who channels these images into the world.

Back Cover: *A New Earth*

"We are unknown, we knowers, ourselves to ourselves: this has its own good reason. We have never searched for ourselves--how should it then come to pass, that we should ever find ourselves?"
~FRIEDRICH NIETZSCHE

Introduction

What are MINDWORKS?
Carl Jung was a pioneer in the exploration of the unconscious mind.
Dreams, fantasies, myths and free associations were some of his tools
of exploration. Calming his mind and allowing thoughts and fantasies
to rise up to consciousness were part of the process. MINDWORKS are
drawing meditations, images rising from the unconscious mind.

'Allowing' is most important. It is necessary to have no pre-conceived
ideas about what the work will be. I start with my mind in an 'idle'
state, kind of drifting, calm and relaxed. I put down a few smudges
with charcoal on paper and ideas rising from my unconscious begin to
appear. I read into these vague marks whatever images come to mind
and then enhance them with more drawing...'drawing' them forth, so
to speak. Associations occur and it is mostly a process of discovery
and adventure. It is important not to judge too quickly, just observe
what is happening. There is no need to control, allowing is the key. It is
very exciting. I let things happen--an advent.

Others have explored similar processes: Max Ernest with collage and
frottage; Odilon Redon who could not abide a blank white surface,
made smudges and saw a butterfly wing; Dubuffet who often began a
canvas not knowing whether it would be a cow, a table or a person;
Leonardo da Vinci who urged us to look at clouds and stains on the
walls and read into them faces, animals and battle-scenes.

MINDWORKS are drawing meditations, a process of discovery, art put
to the service of self-realization for the artist as well as the viewer.

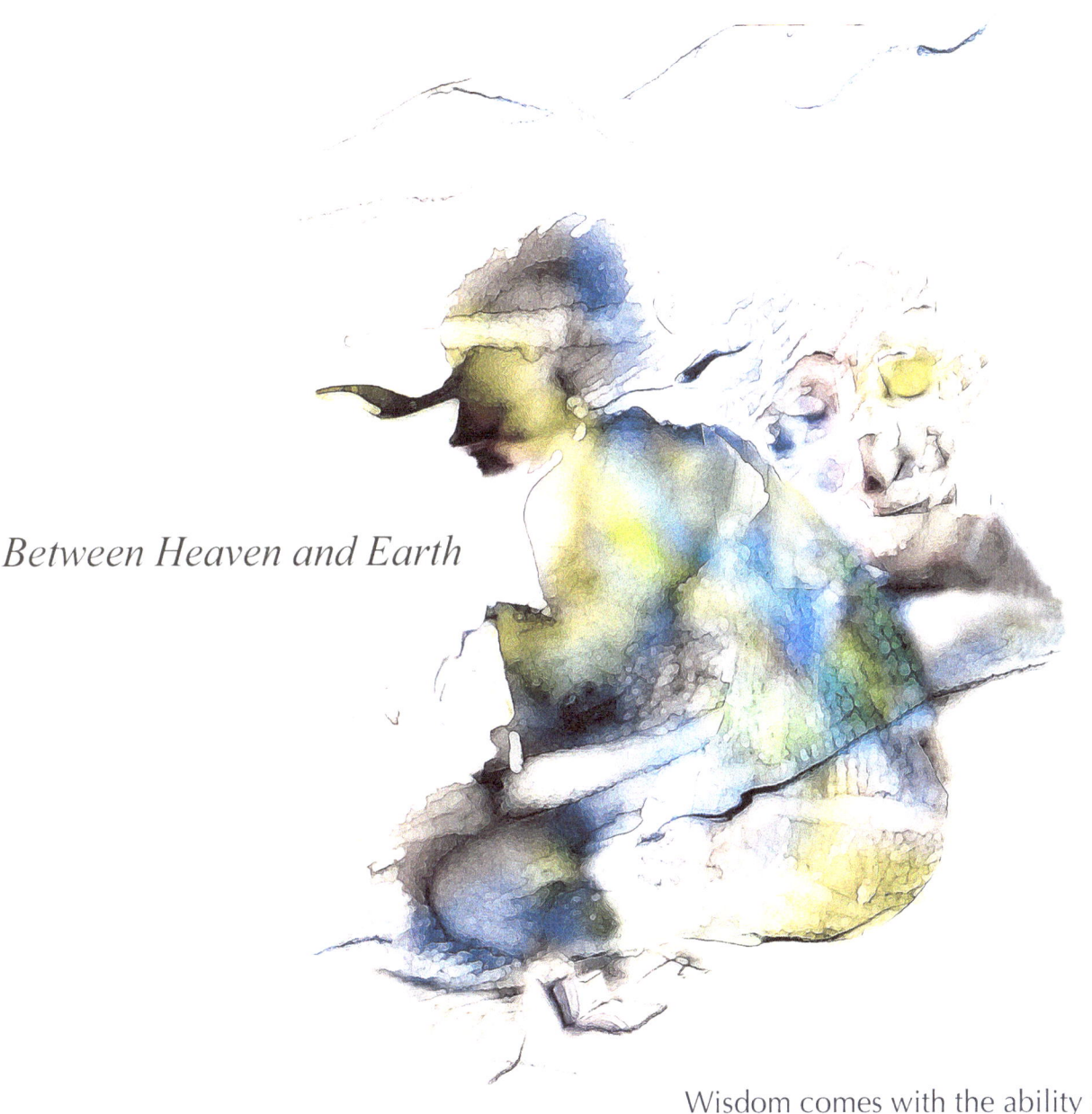

Between Heaven and Earth

Wisdom comes with the ability to
be still. Just look and just listen.
No more is needed.
~ECKHART TOLLE, *Stillness Speaks, 2003*

1

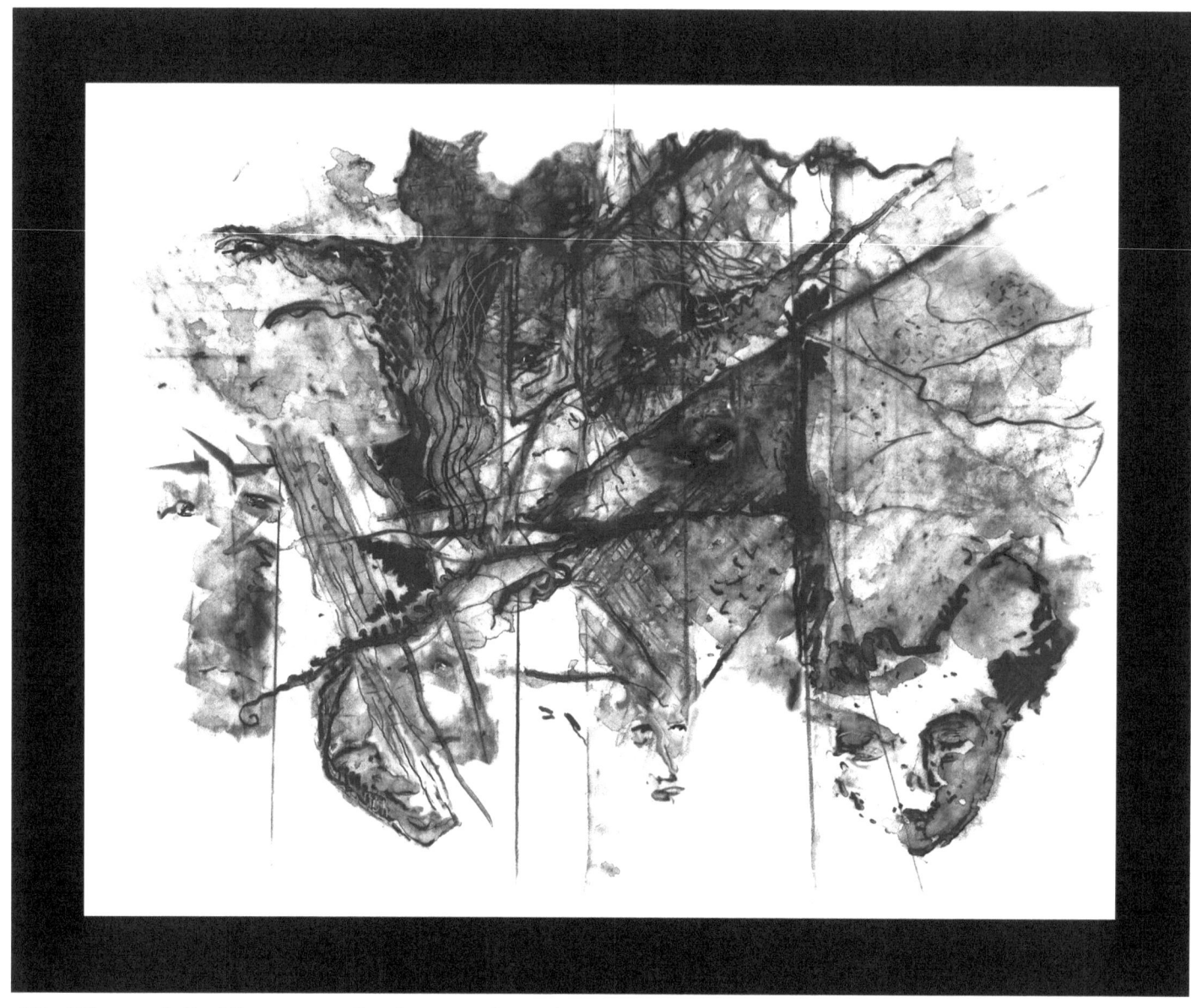

"I Close My Eyes in Order to See." ~PAUL GAUGUIN

Paul Gauguin said don't paint
what you SEE but what you
KNOW about what you see.

2

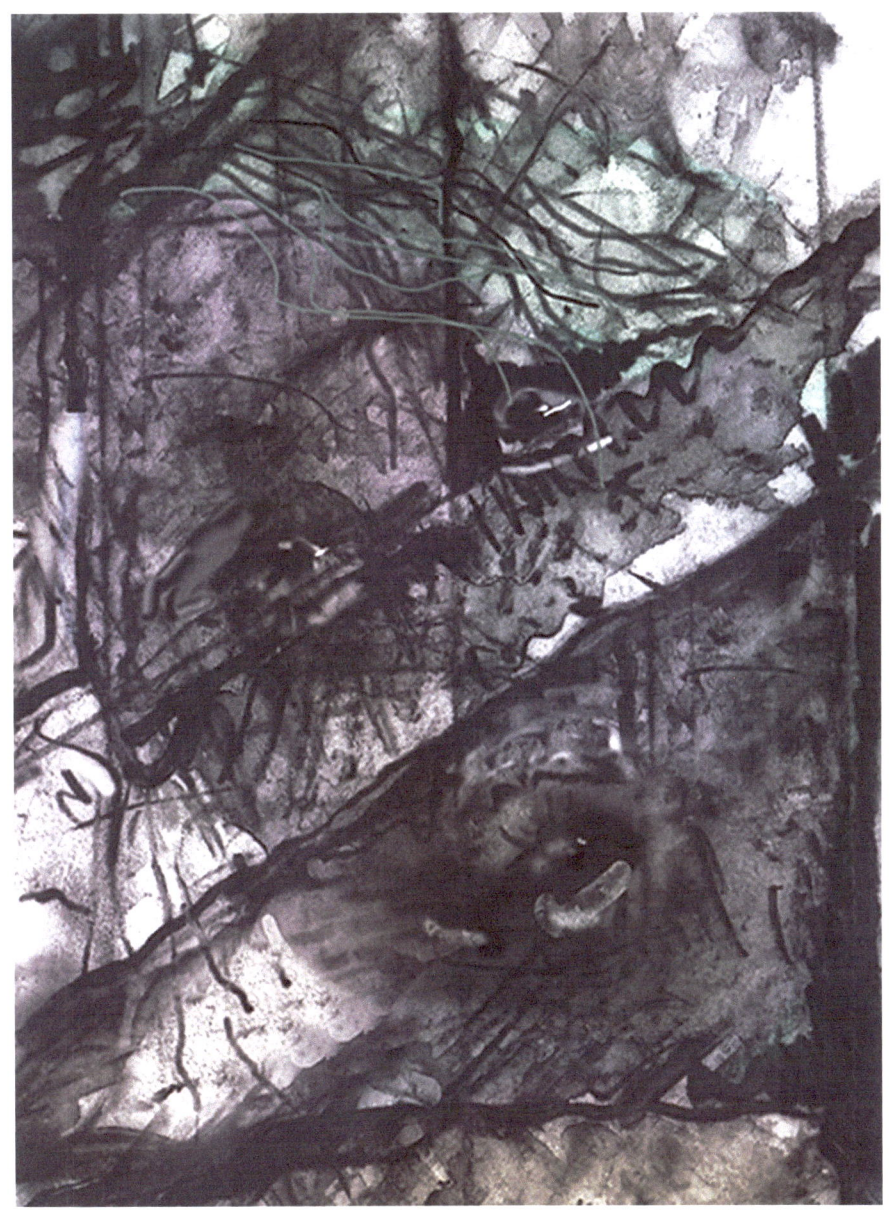

Detail

"Close both eyes to see with the other eye." ~RUMI

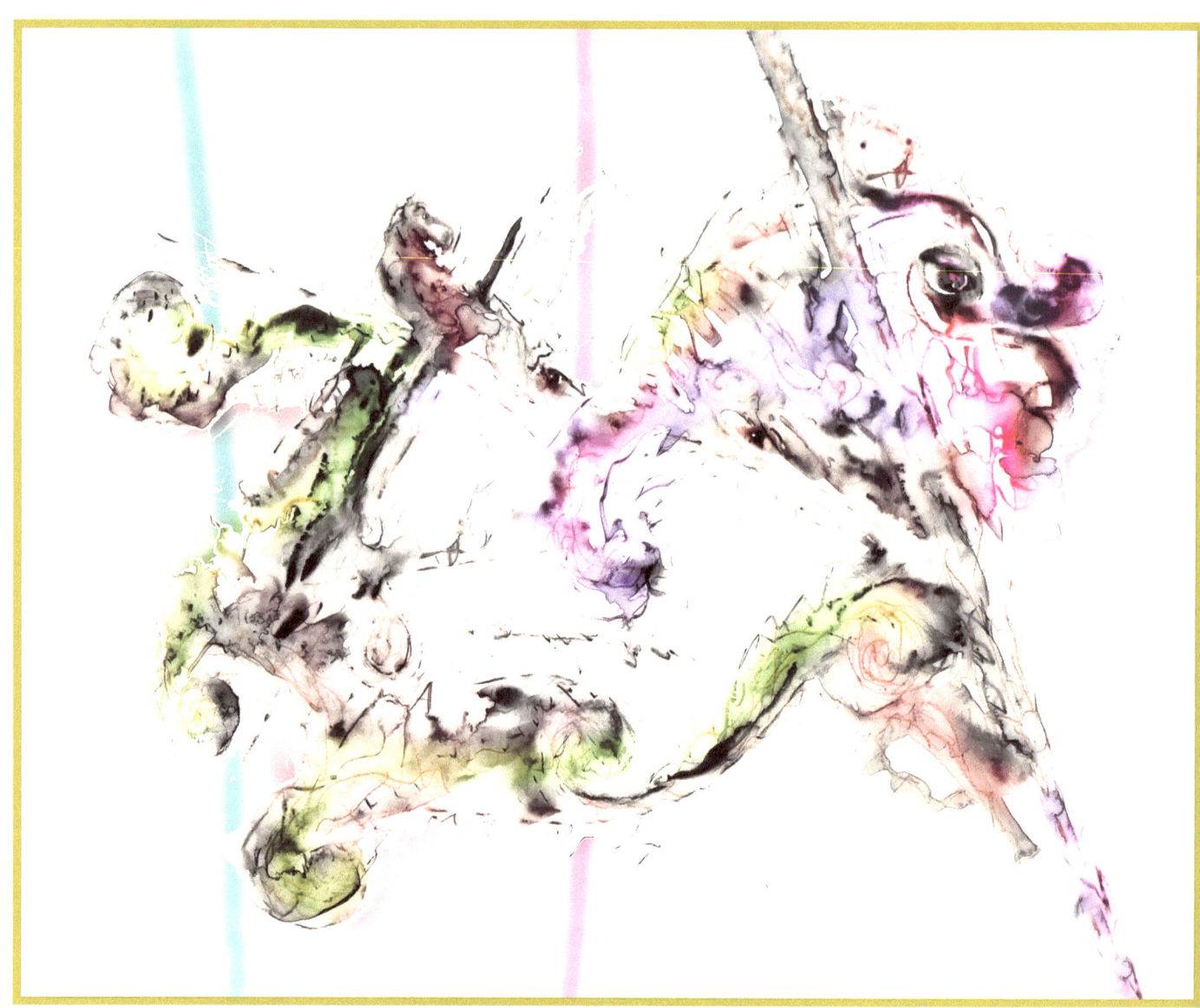

Carousel Man

You imagine who you are.
What could be more intimate
and creative?

Cosmic Dance

When you are aware
of being aware, things
lose their seriousness,
their heaviness. Life
becomes playful; the
world is seen as a
cosmic dance.

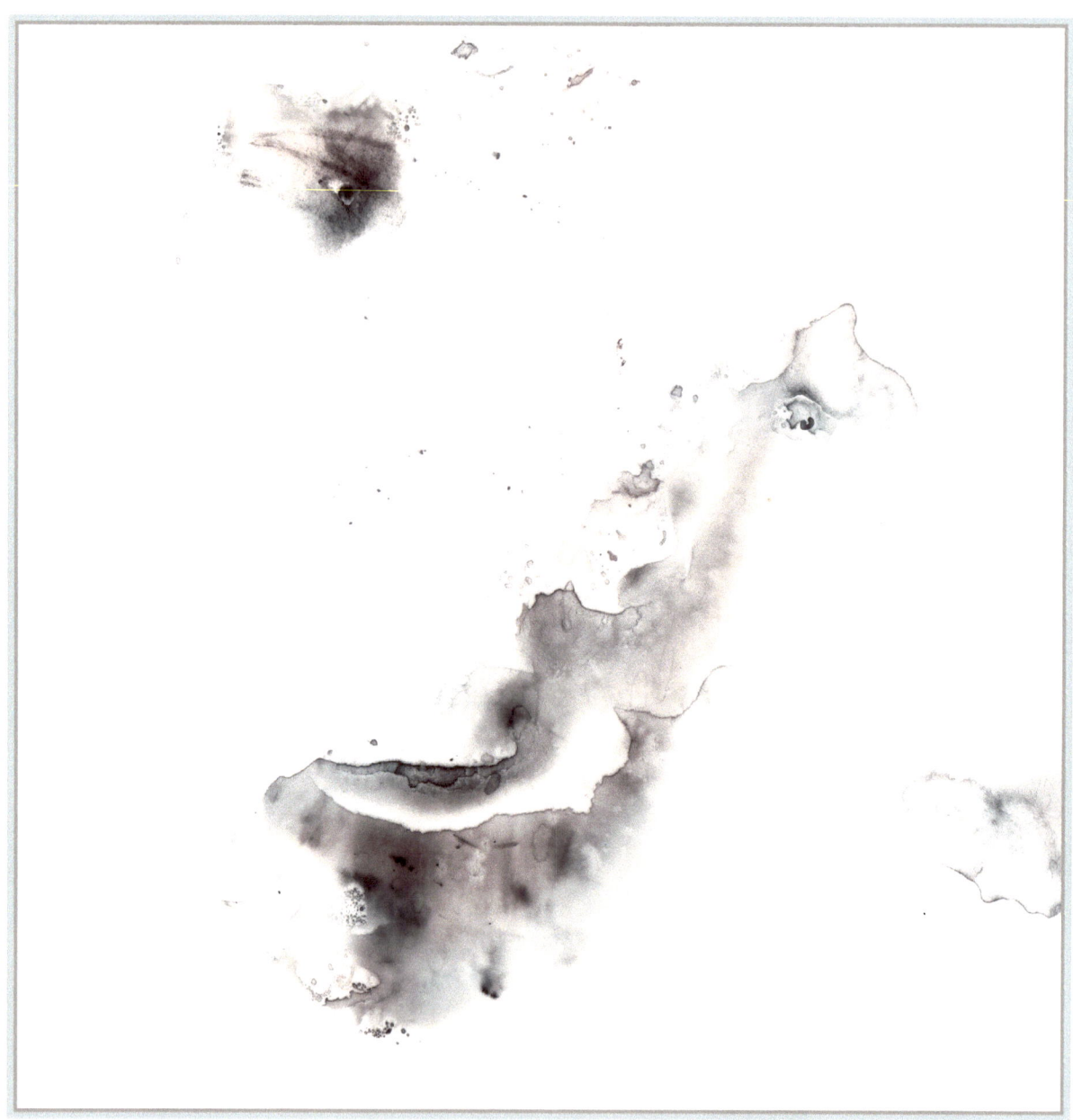

Mastery in whatever we undertake -- art, dance, teaching, sports -- is being aligned with a greater consciousness. It acts, speaks and does the work. It is necessary to have no pre-conceived ideas about what the work will be. Be the Silent Witness.

"At some stage in the process of creation the creative product--whether painting, poem, or scientific theory--takes on a life of its own and transmits its own needs to its creator. It stands apart from him and summons material from his subconscious. The creator, then, must know when to cease directing his work and when to allow it to direct him. He must know, in short, when his work is likely to be wiser than he."
~GEORGE KNELLER,*The Art and Science of Creativity,1965*

"The songs made me, not I them."~GOETHE

Being Aware of Awareness

Inner stillness, peace, is possible for each of us by becoming fully aware of all we perceive, think and feel.

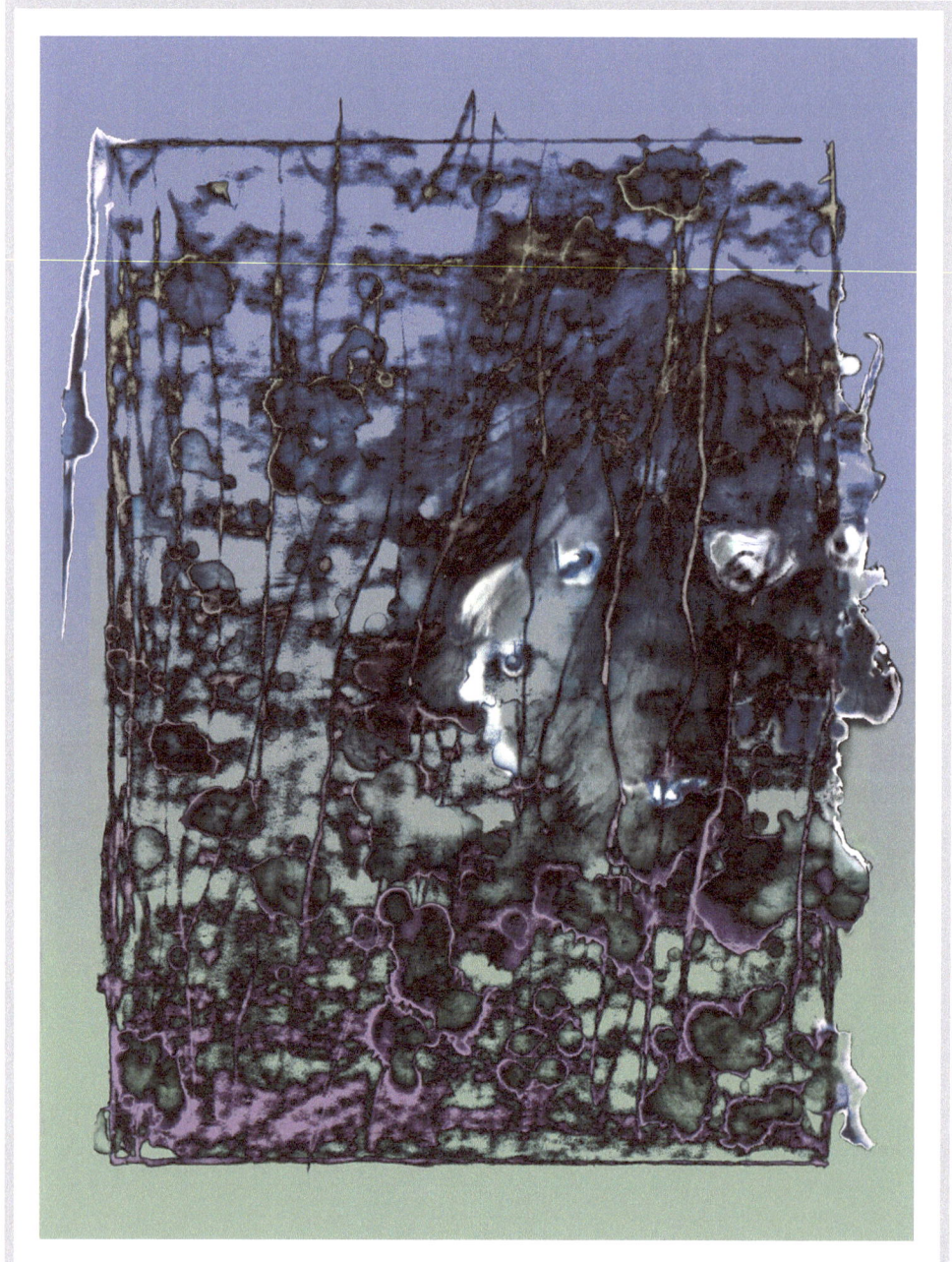

Damn! Angry Again
-variation 3

"Man needs reckless
courage to descend
into the abyss of
himself."~YEATS

8

Fearful

"As long as the ego runs your life, most of your thoughts, emotions, and actions arise from desire and fear. In relationships you then either want or fear something from the other person."
~ECKHART TOLLE,
Stillness Speaks, 2003

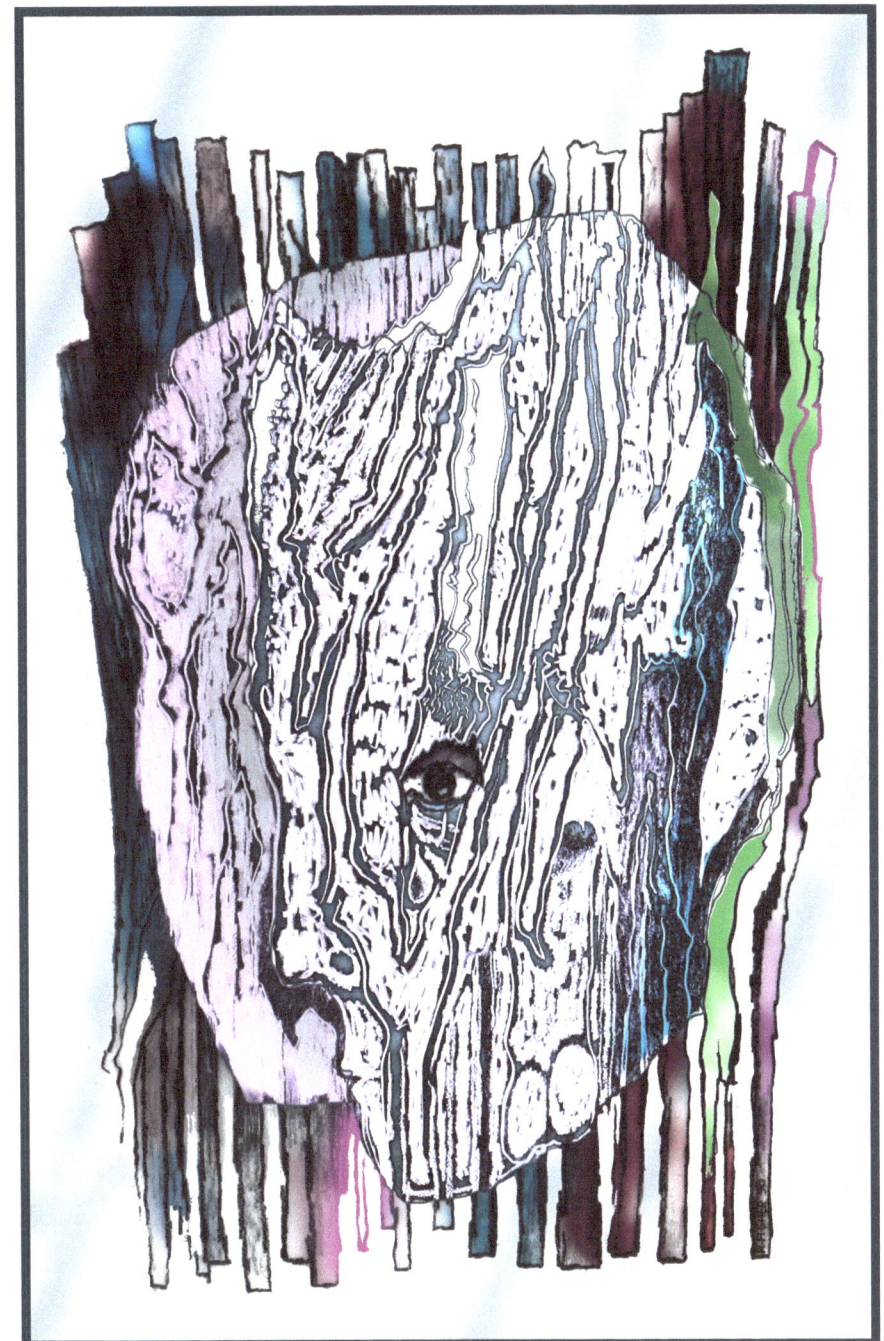

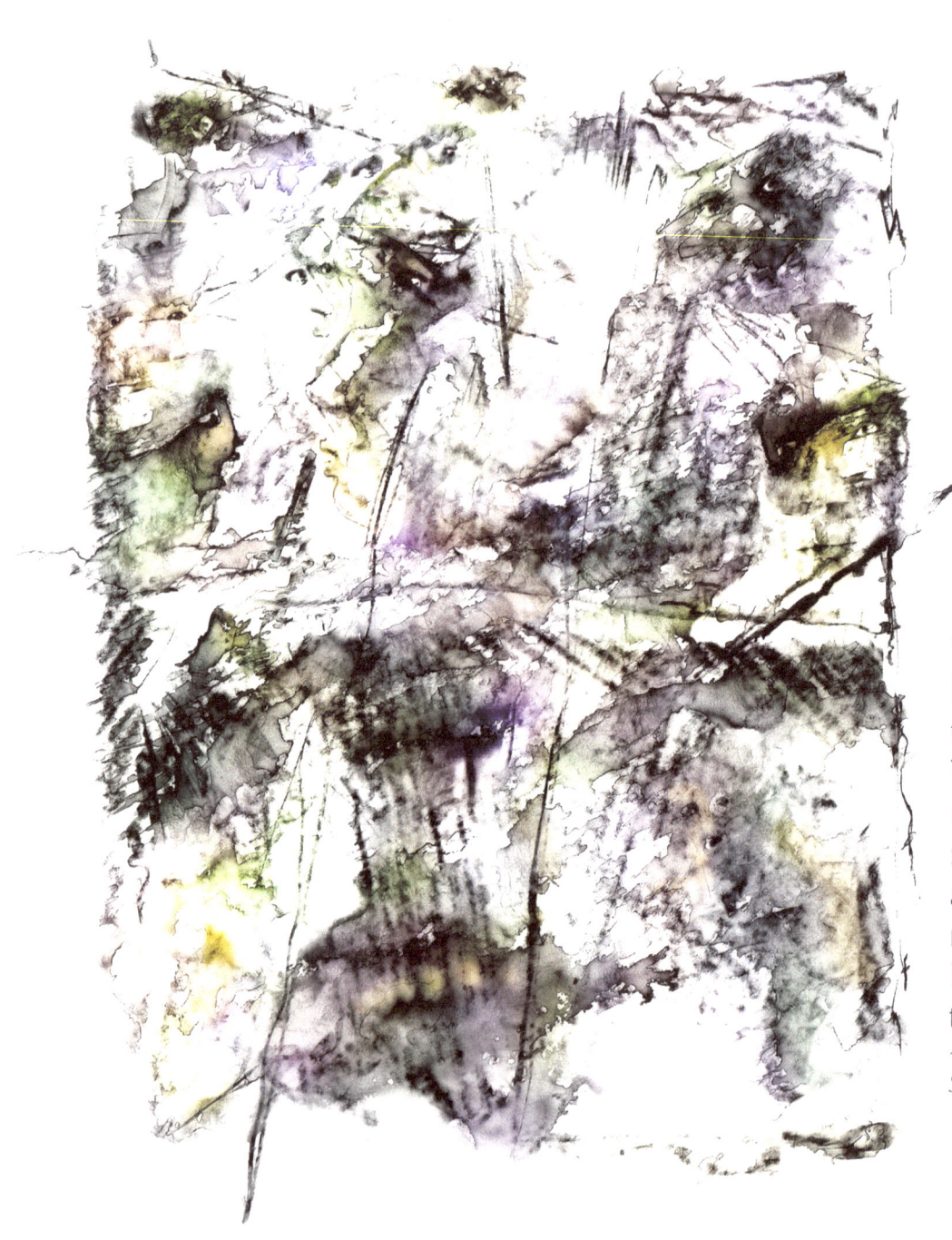

Ego Chatter

"The next step in human evolution is to transcend thought. This is now our urgent task. It doesn't mean not to think anymore, but simply not to be completely identified with thought."
~ECKHART TOLLE,
Stillness Speaks, 2003

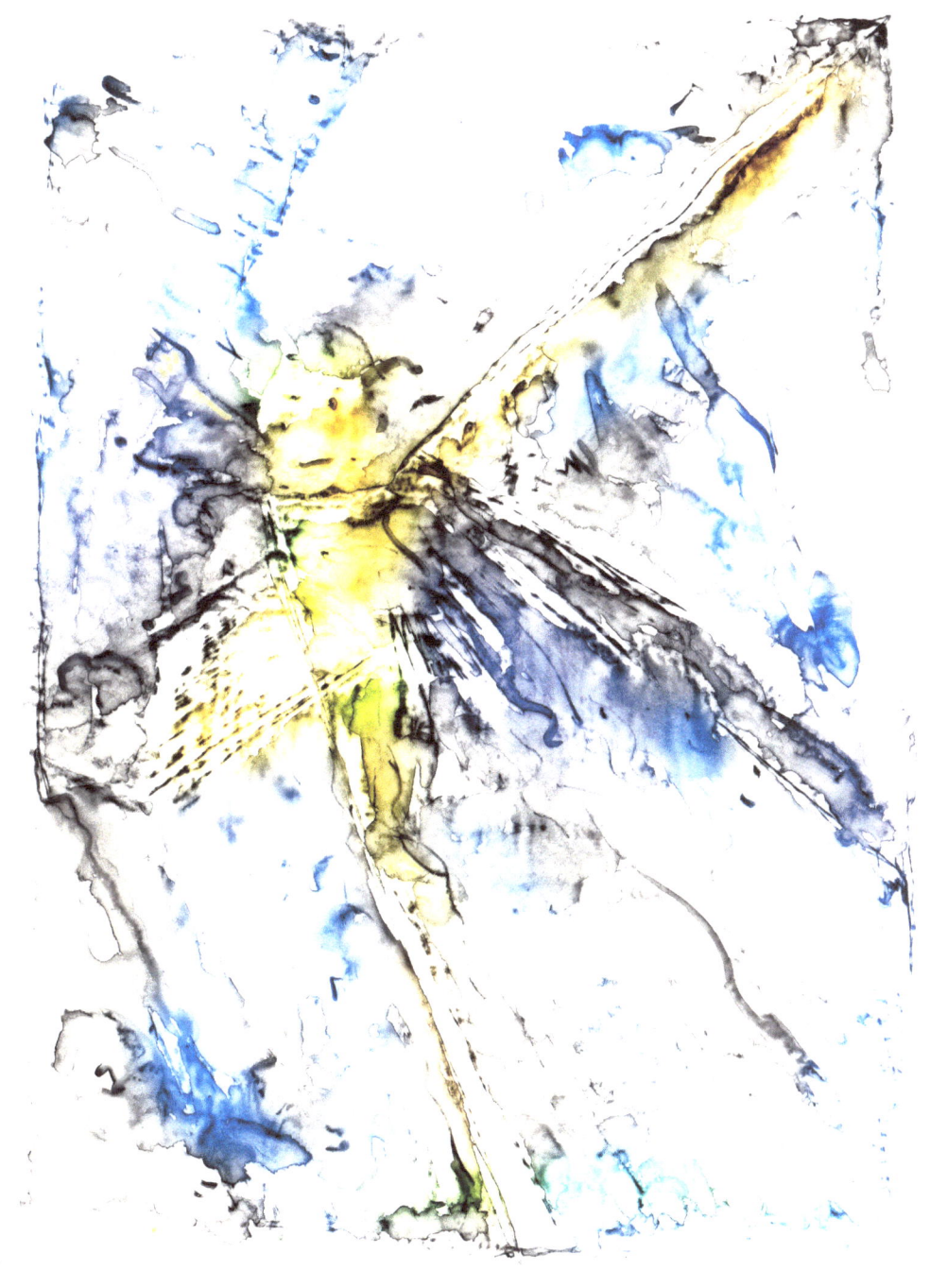

Dan Takes to the Sky on his Home-made Wings

"I asked for a kiss, you gave me six. Whose pupil were you to become such a master? Full of kindness, generosity... You are not of this world." ~RUMI

11

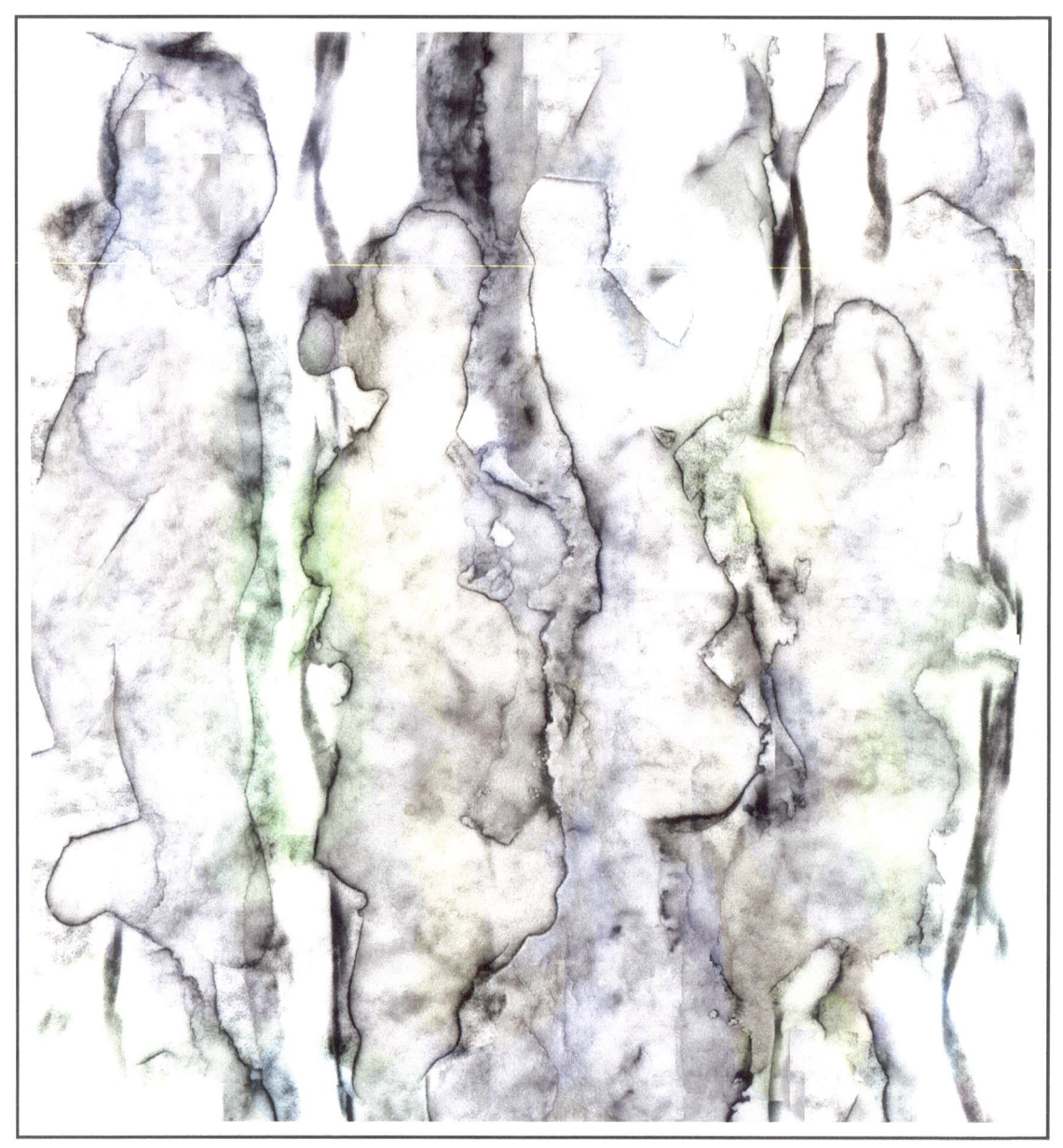

Dancers

"We rarely hear the inward music,
but we're all dancing to it nevertheless." ~RUMI

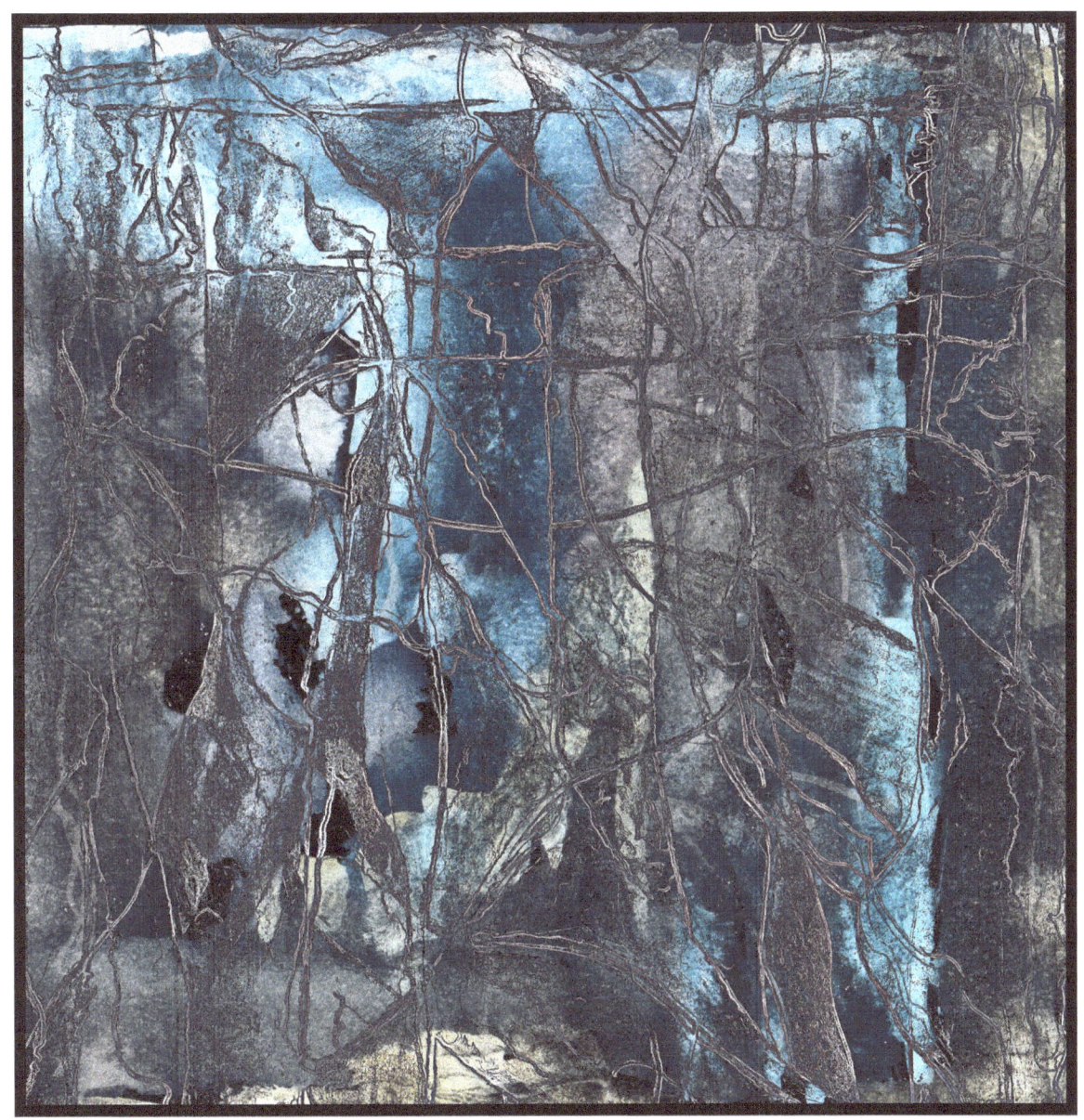

Forest Secrets

"Understand the art of Allowing... the path of least resistance." ~WAYNE DYER

13

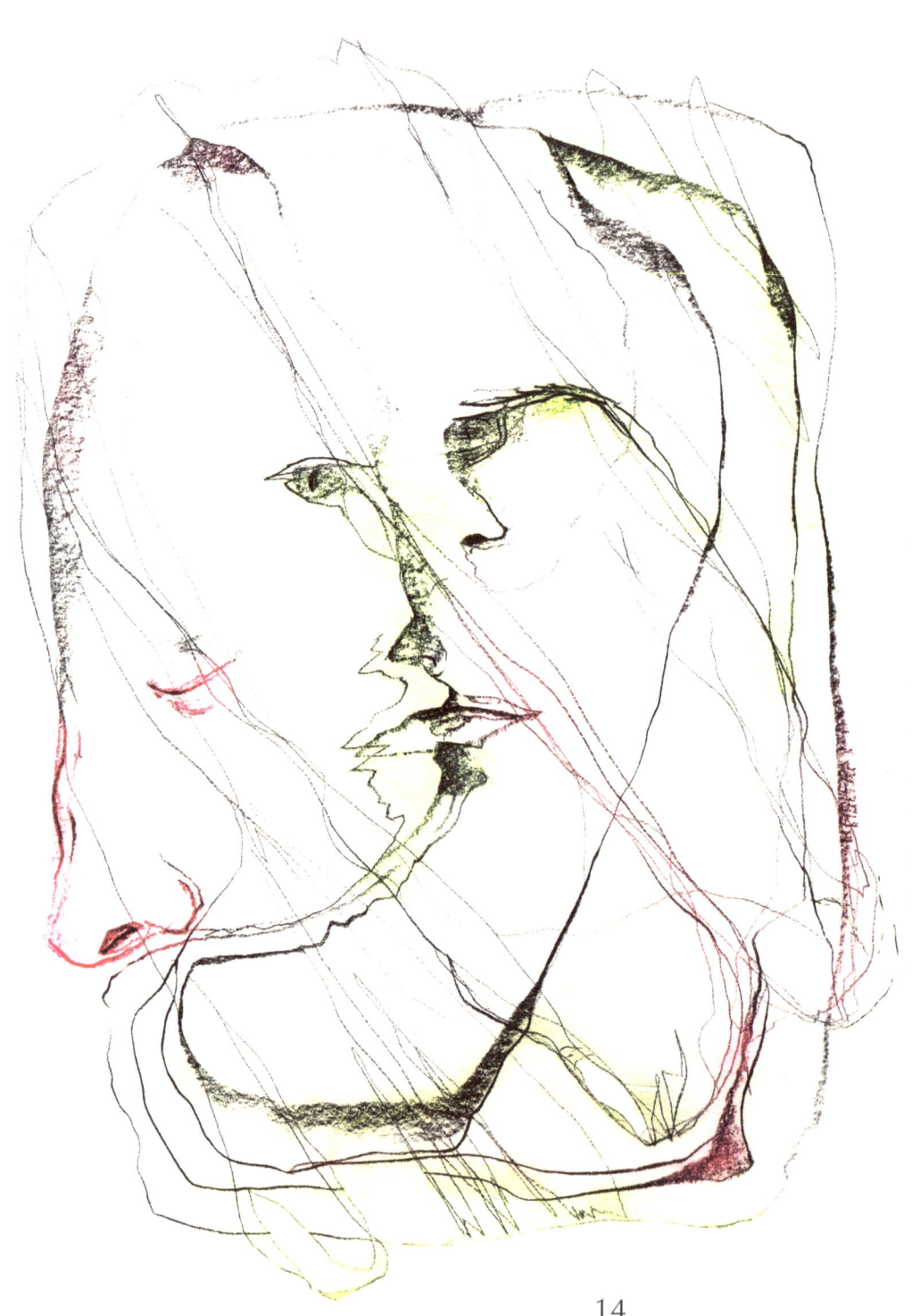

Forgetting

"There is a spiritual
awakening that we
are beginning to
witness now...a shift
in consciousness...
a new Earth."
~ECKHART TOLLE,
A New Earth, 2005

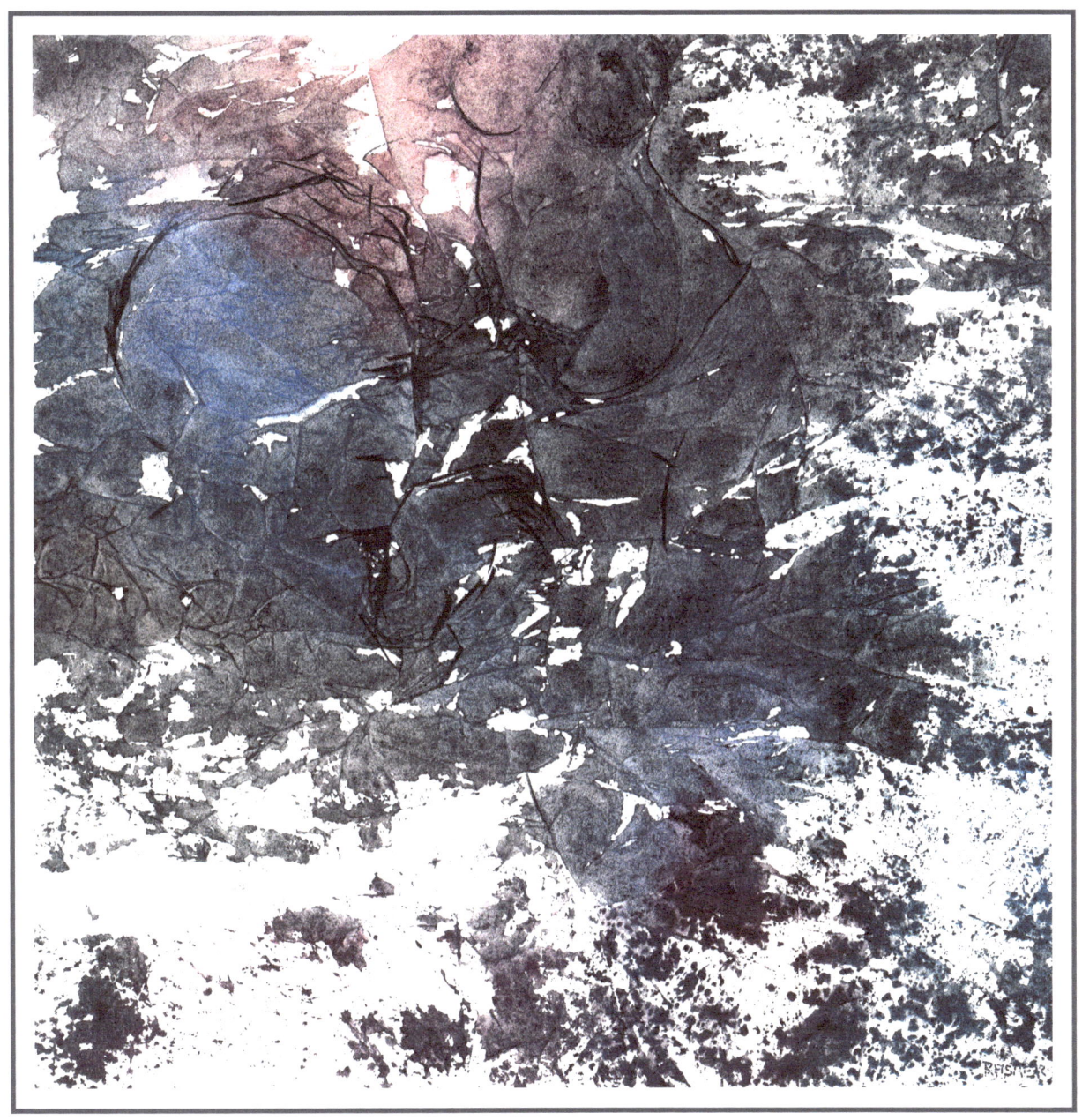

Desire

"When your passion awakens, your soul becomes young and free and dances again...true vitality is hidden within longing."
~JOHN O'DONOHUE, *Anam Cara, a Book of Celtic Wisdom.*1997

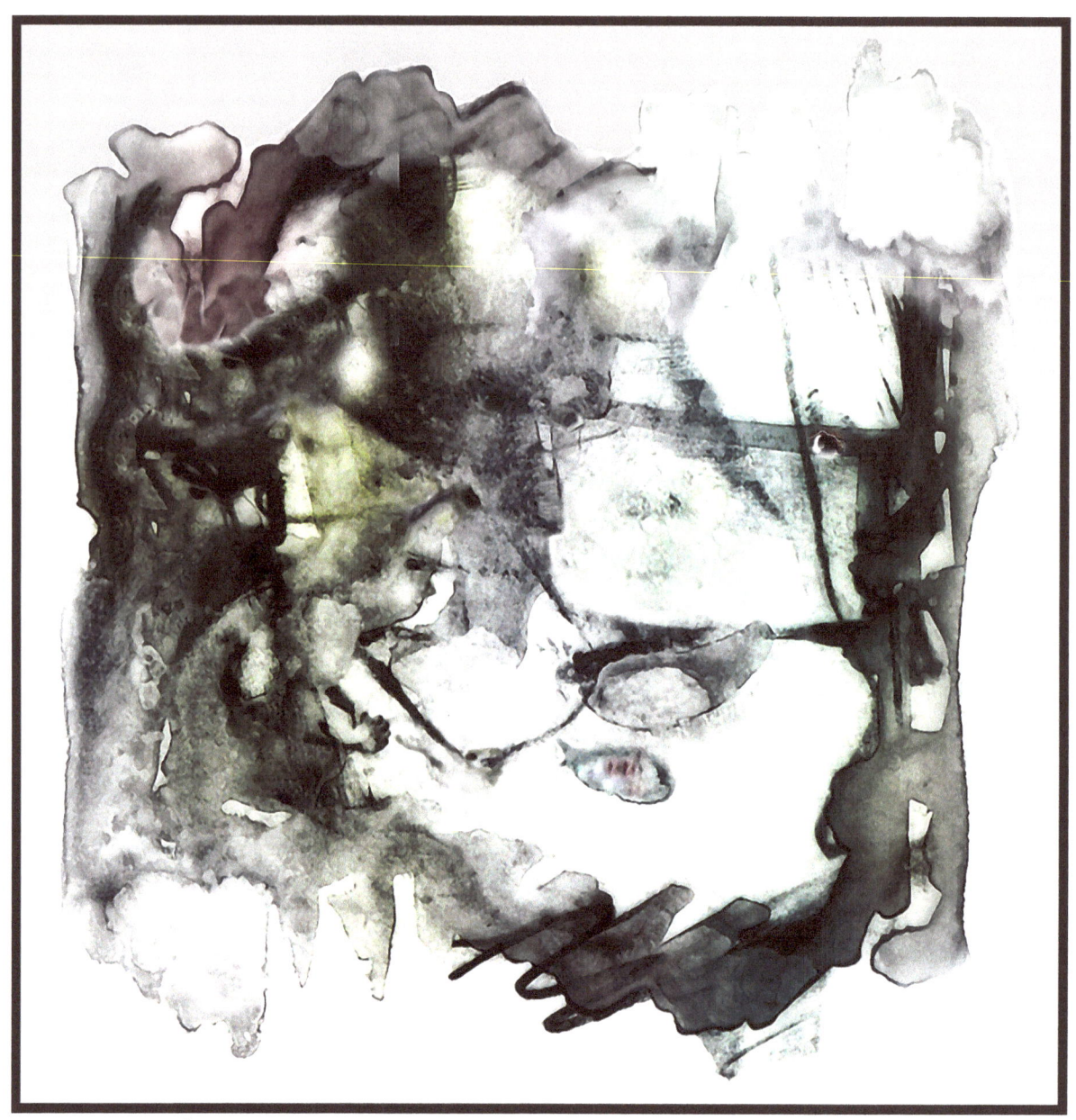

Gone Fishing

"The position of the artist is humble. He is essentially a channel." ~PIET MONDRIAN

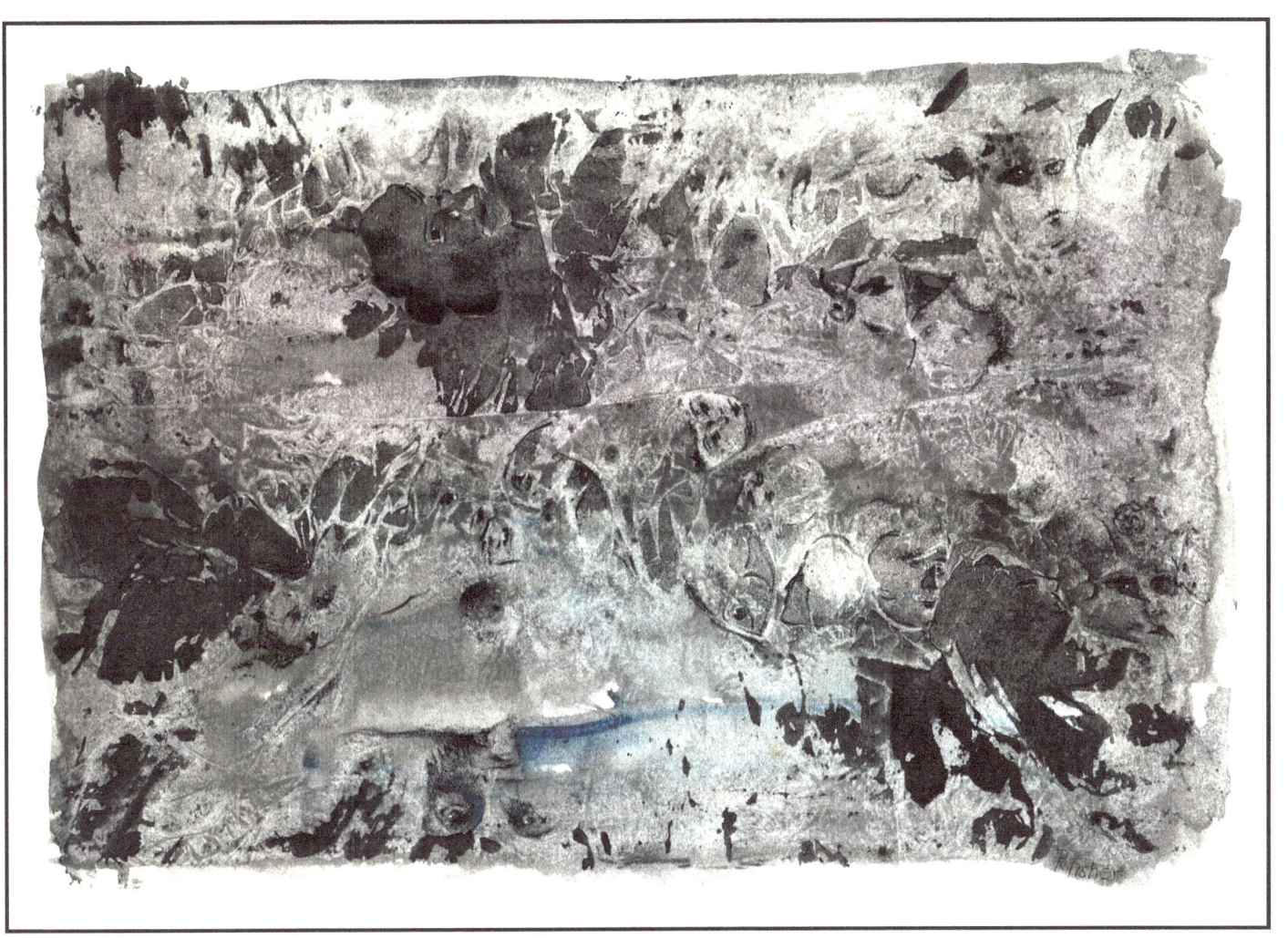

InnerScape

The inner world of our minds is a landscape
which conceals a vast presence. It's shape is an
ancient and silent form of consciousness.
~JOHN O'DONOHUE, *Anam Cara, a Book of Celtic Wisdom, 1997*

"The imagination works through suggestion, not
description. Description is always direct and frequently
closes off what it names. Suggestion respects the
mystery and richness of a thing. All it offers are clues to
its nature. Suggestion keeps the mystery open and
extends us the courtesy of inviting us to see the thing
for ourselves. It offers us the hospitality and freedom to
trust the integrity of our own encounter with a thing.
This is how a work of art can allow itself to be seen in
so many different and often conflicting ways, it does
not foreclose on the adventure of revelation."
~JOHN O'DONOHUE, *Beauty*, 2004

"The essence of the mystery is to preserve a state of
ambivalence, through double and triple possible
interpretations, through mere hints of interpretations
(images within images), through forms that will
materialize, but will do so only in the consciousness
of the spectator." ~ODILON REDON

"The most beautiful thing we can experience is
the mysterious." ~ALBERT EINSTEIN

Gnomes Brothers

You are constantly creating yourself,
deciding who and what you are.

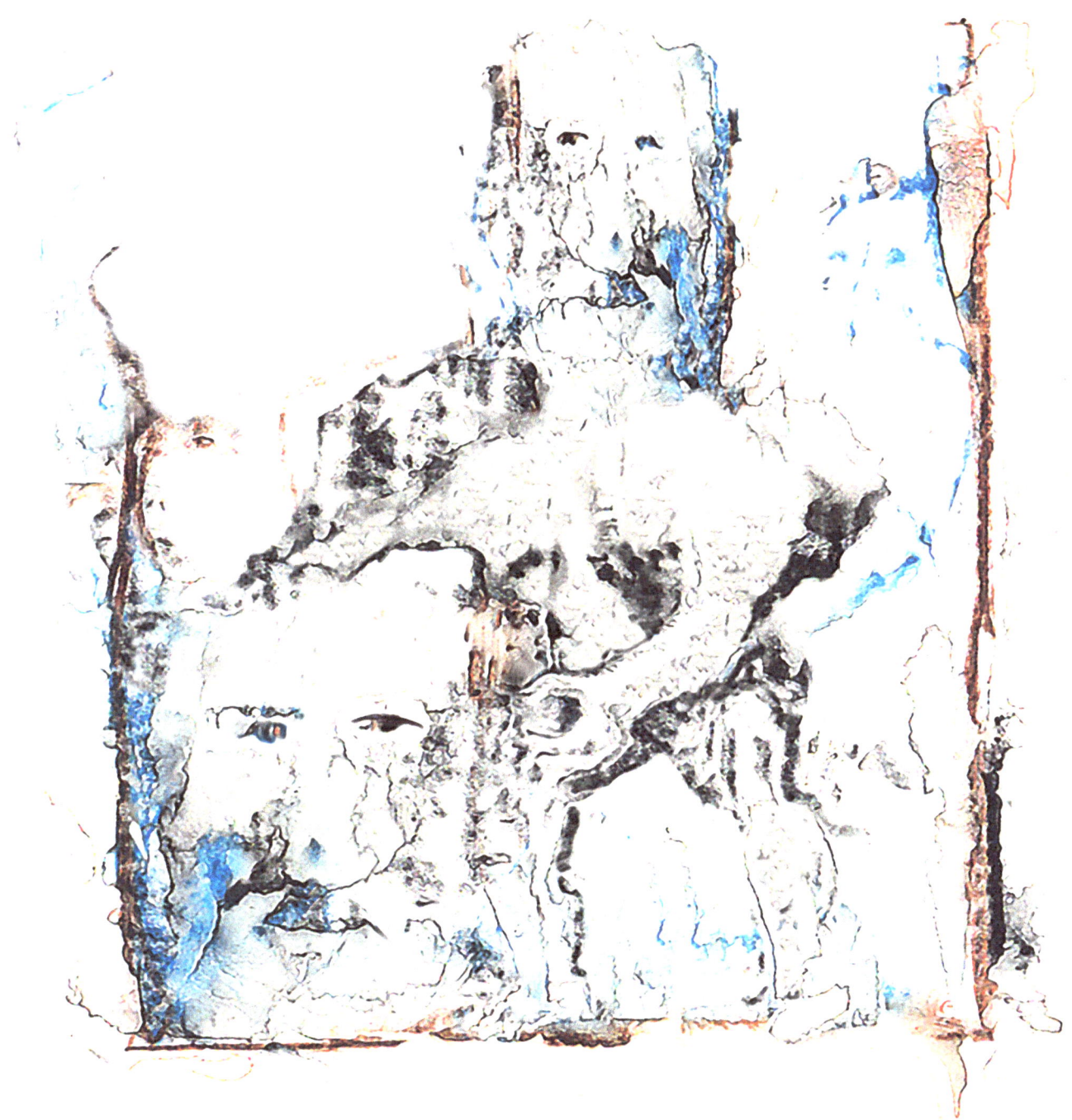

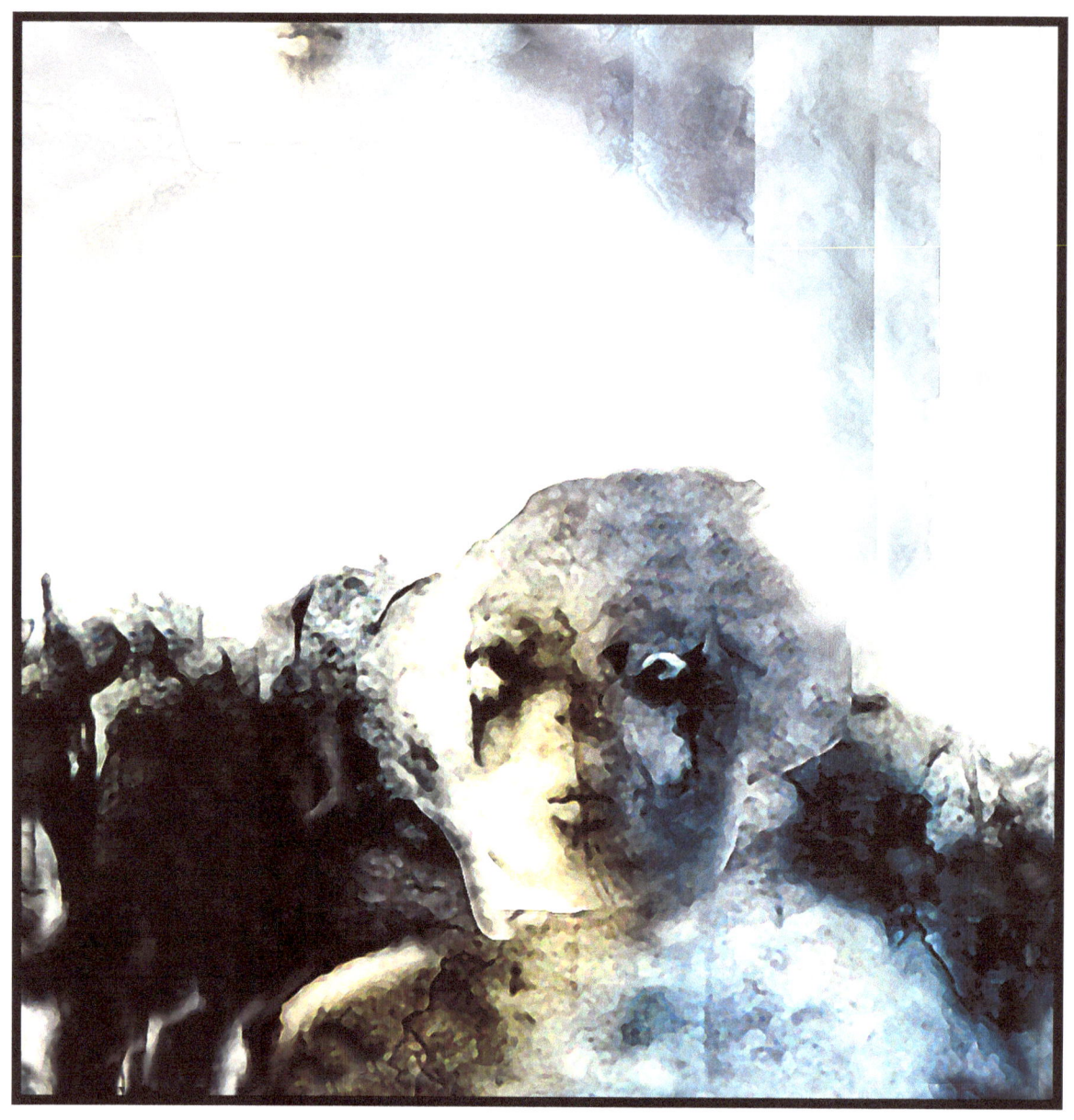

Madness You Say!

"I want to know the mind of God, the rest are details."
ALBERT EINSTEIN

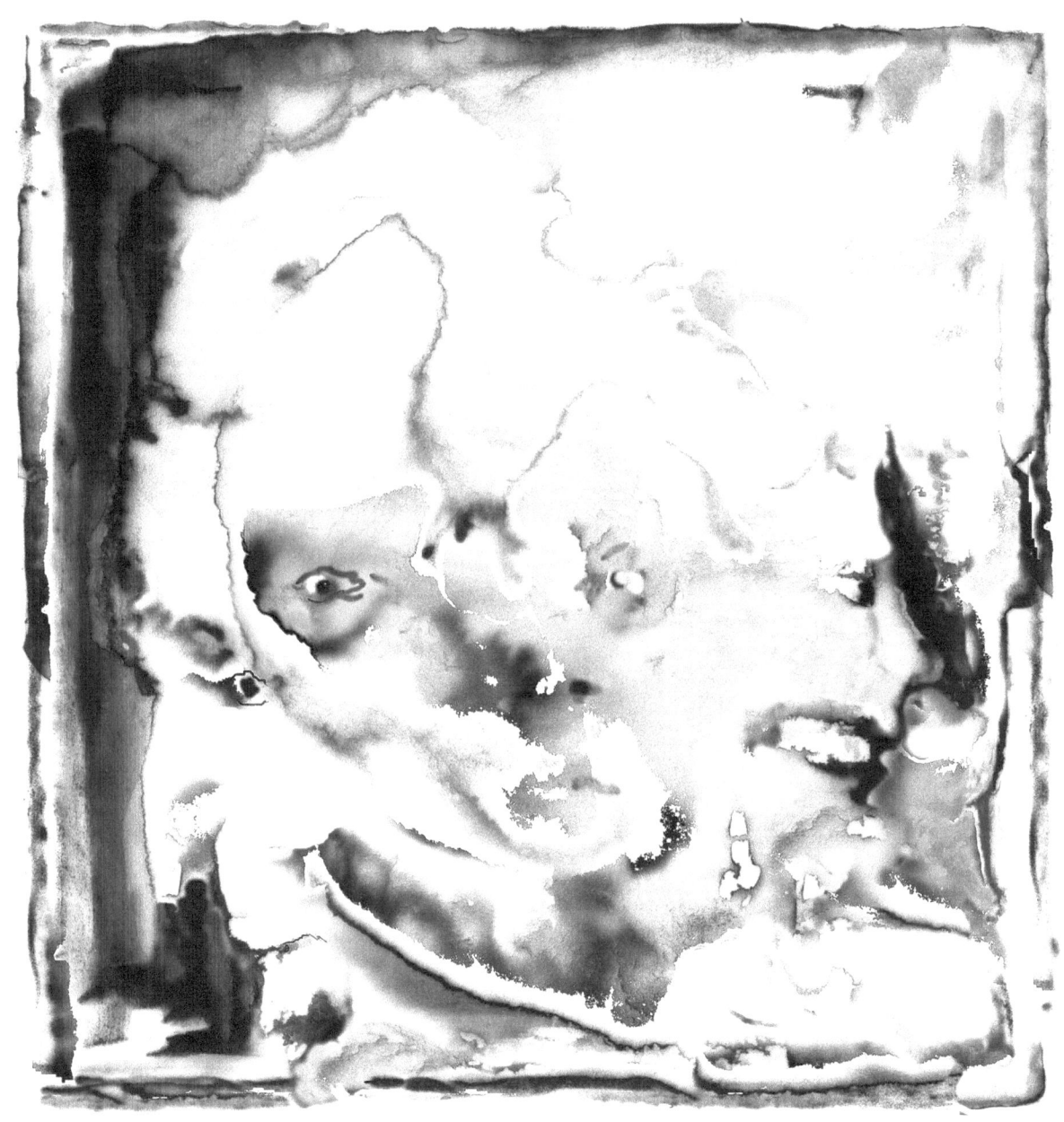

Oh Hell!

"...the voice in my head is not who I am.
Who am I then? The one who sees that."
~ECKHART TOLLE, *A New Earth, 2005*

21

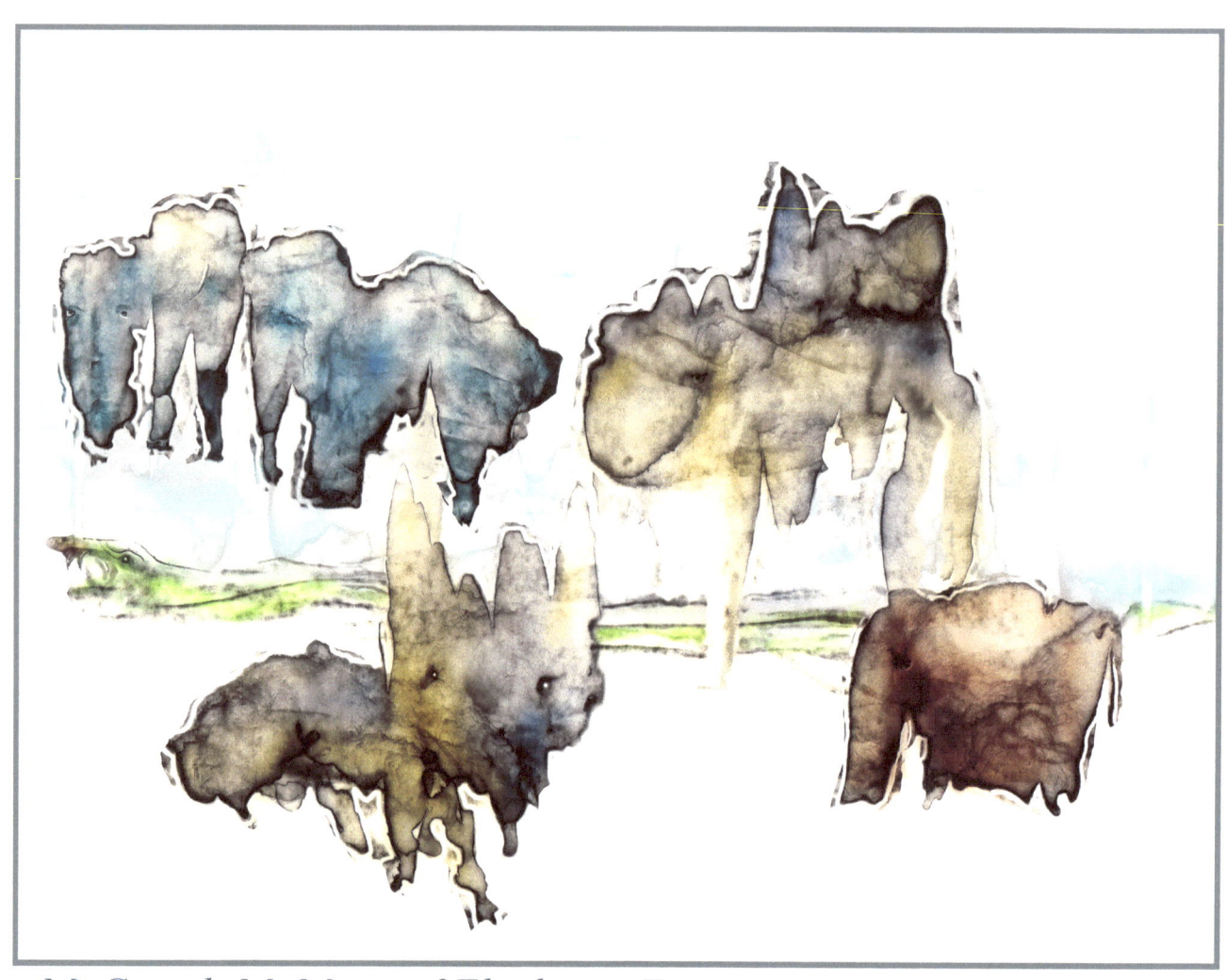

*Mr.Camel, Mr.Mouse, 3Elephants,Esq.
and Mr.Snake*

"The job of the artist is
always to deepend the mystery"
~FRANCIS BACON

Metamorphosis

Transcendence
is at the heart of
our being and a
challenge for
each of us.

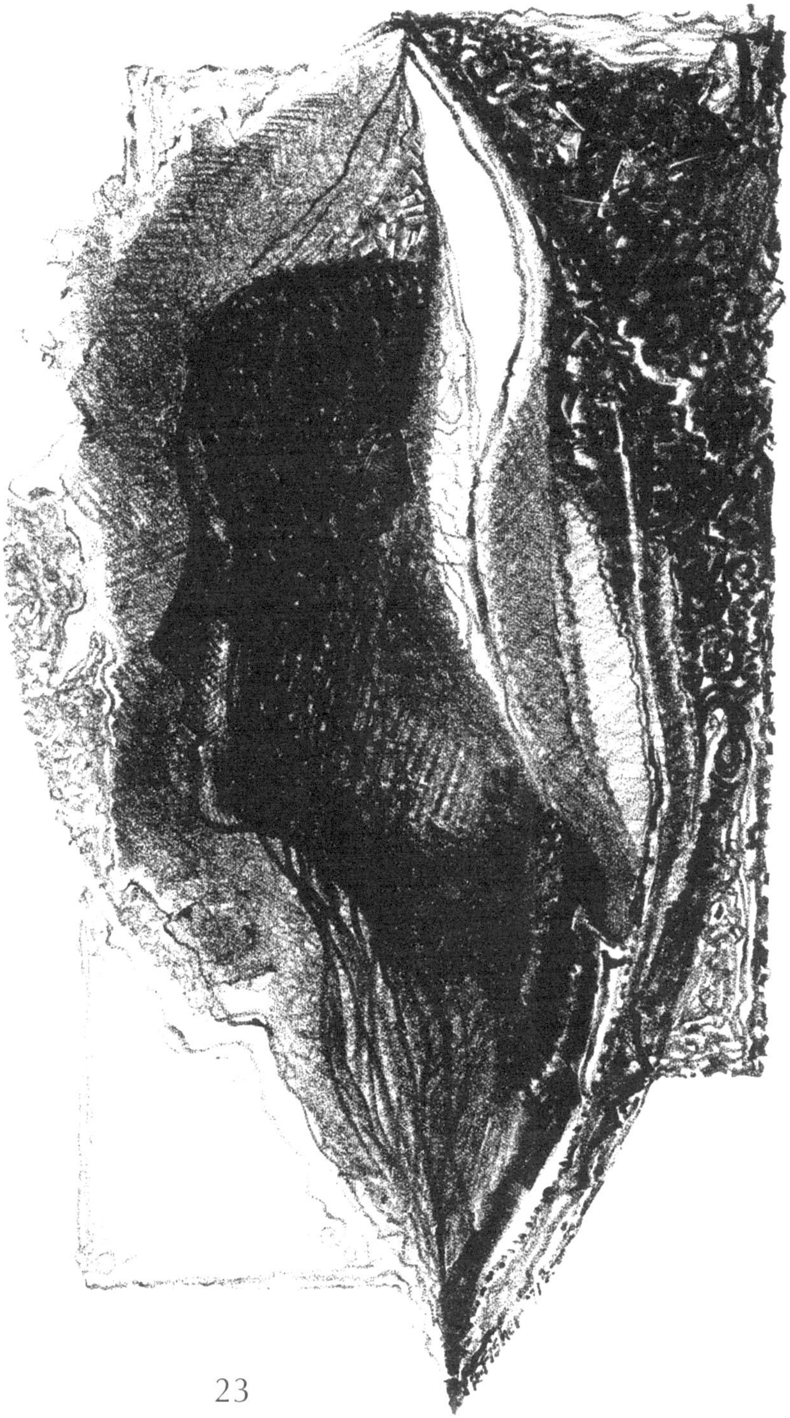

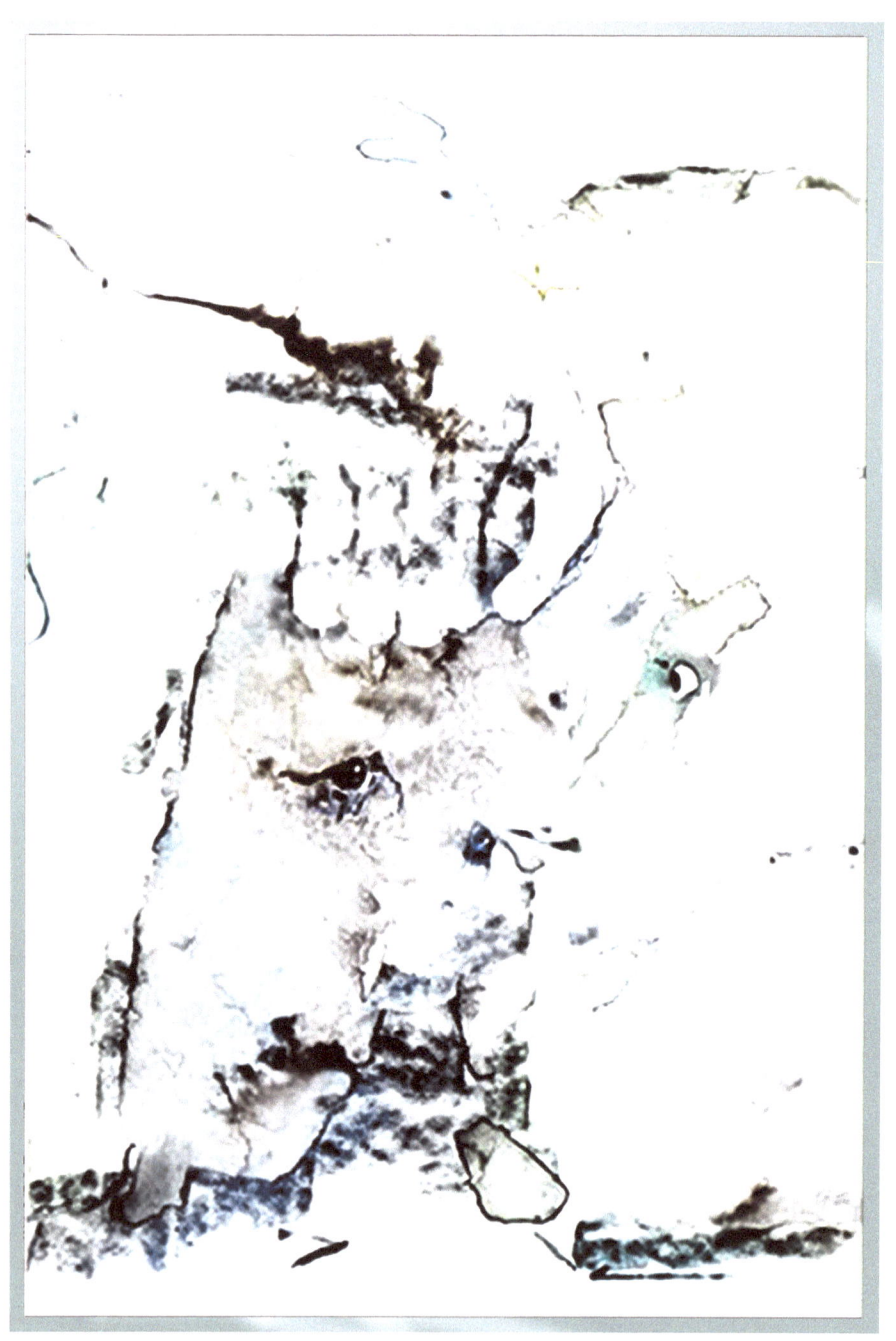

Sheltering

"To see the World
in a Grain of sand
And Heaven
in a Wild Flower,
Hold Infinity in
the palm of your hand
And Eternity in an hour."
~WILLIAM BLAKE,
Auguries of Innocence

Timid One

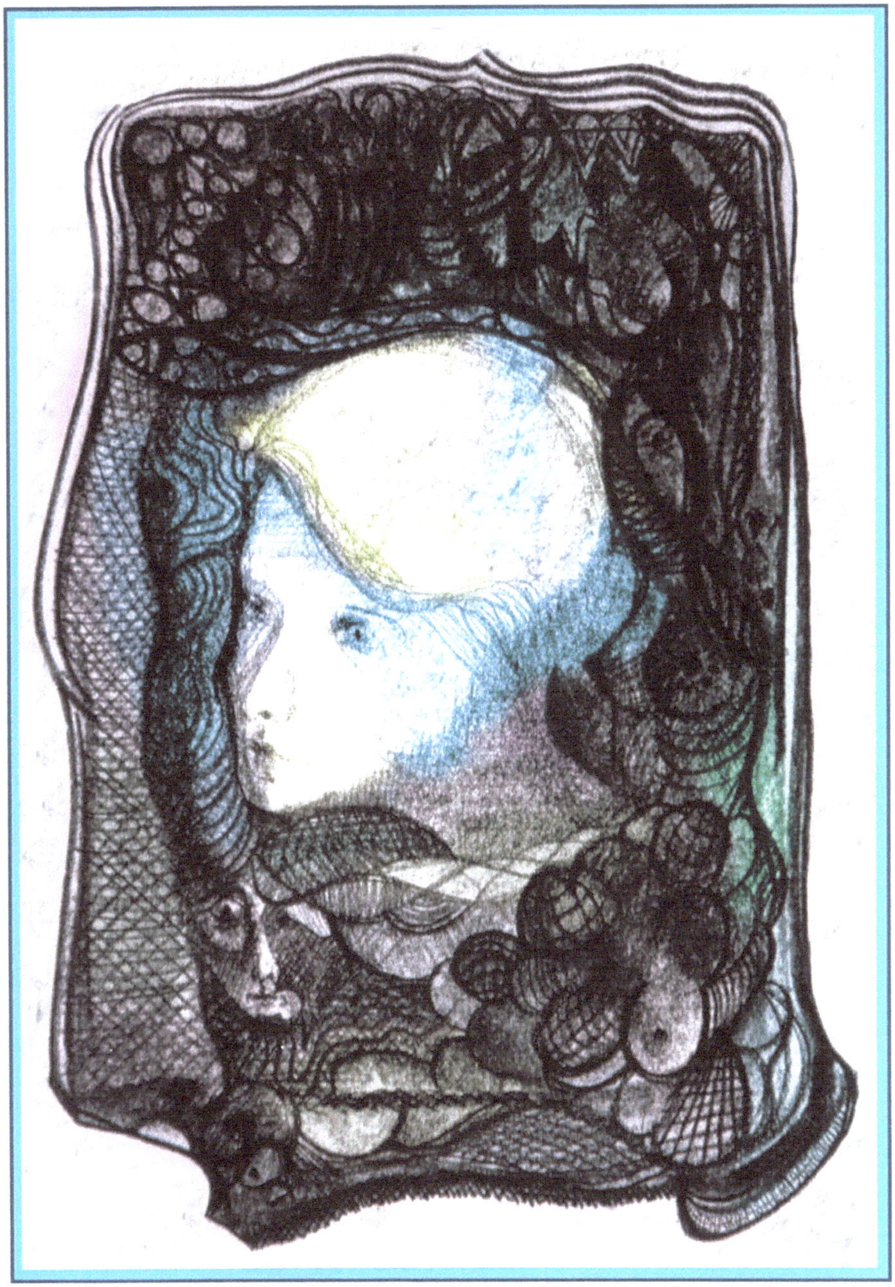

"I" "me" "mine"
"myself" "ours"
"theirs" -- all
create a sense of
separateness, an
illusory sense of
identity, the ego.
~ECKHART TOLLE,
A New Earth, 2005

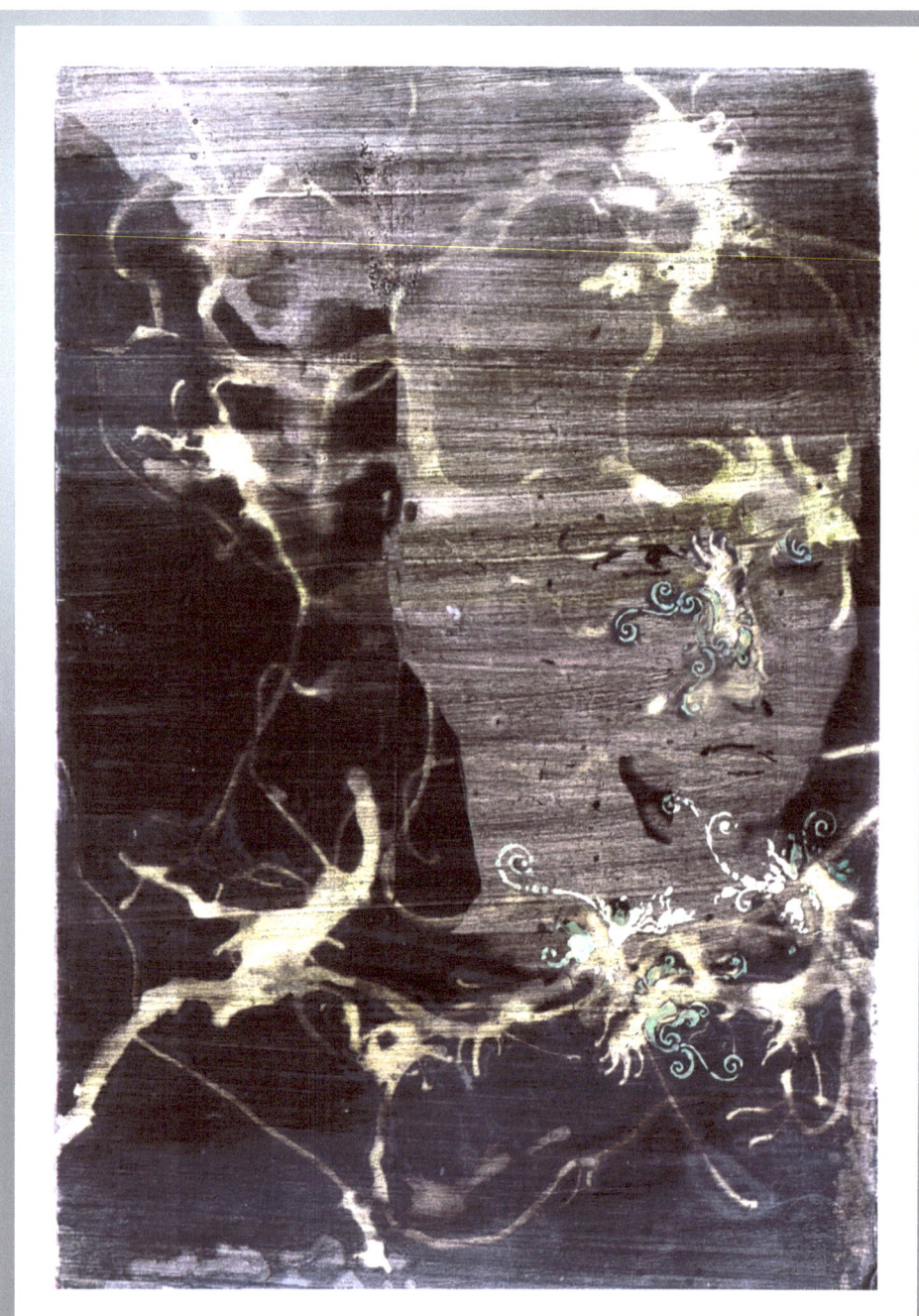

Self-Creating

"Why should I seek?
I am the same as he.
His essence speaks
through me.
I have been looking
for myself!" ~RUMI

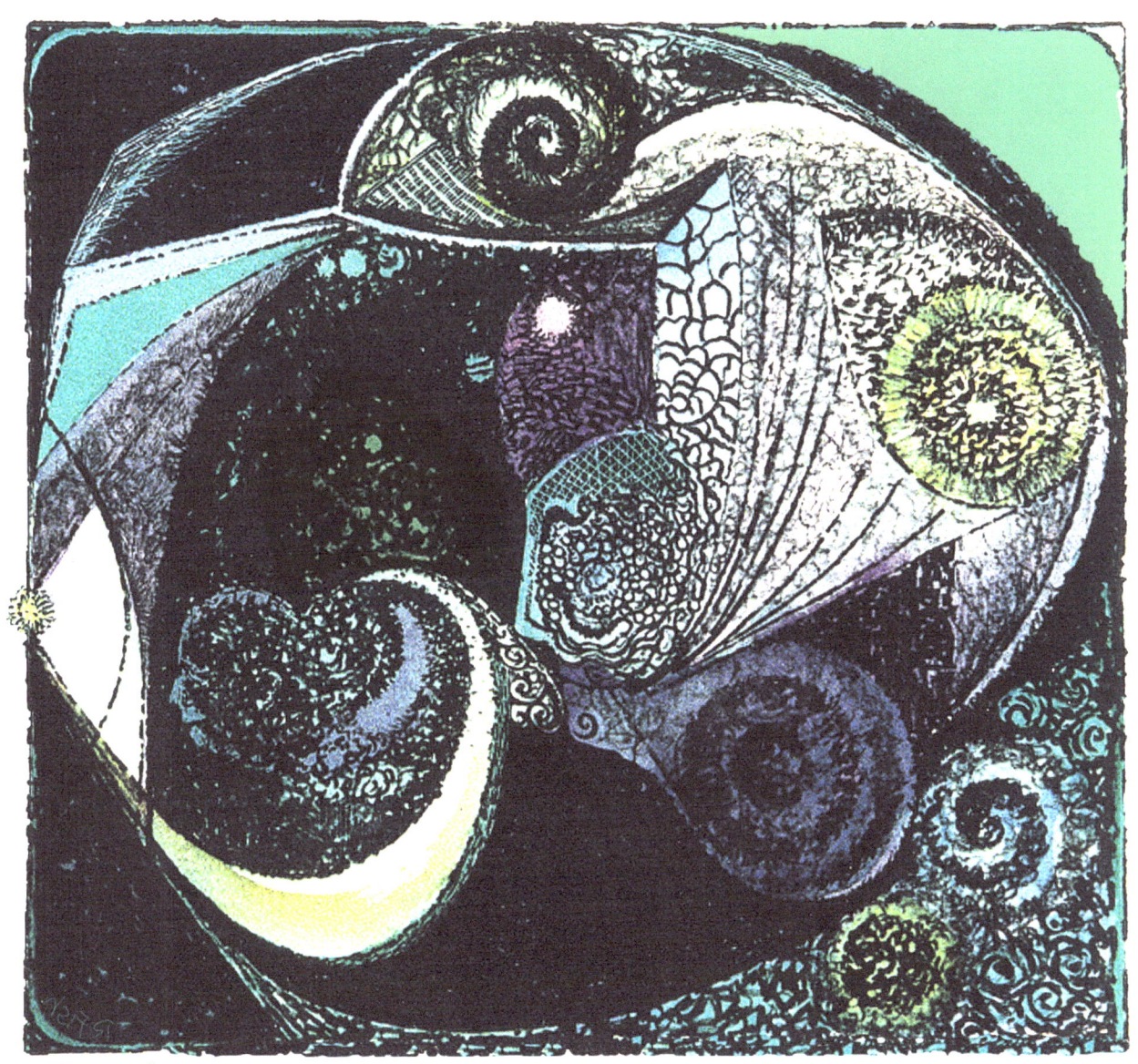

Time Traveler

This image has a sub-title:
"...and there I travel, looking, looking breathlessly."
~CARLOS CASTANEDA

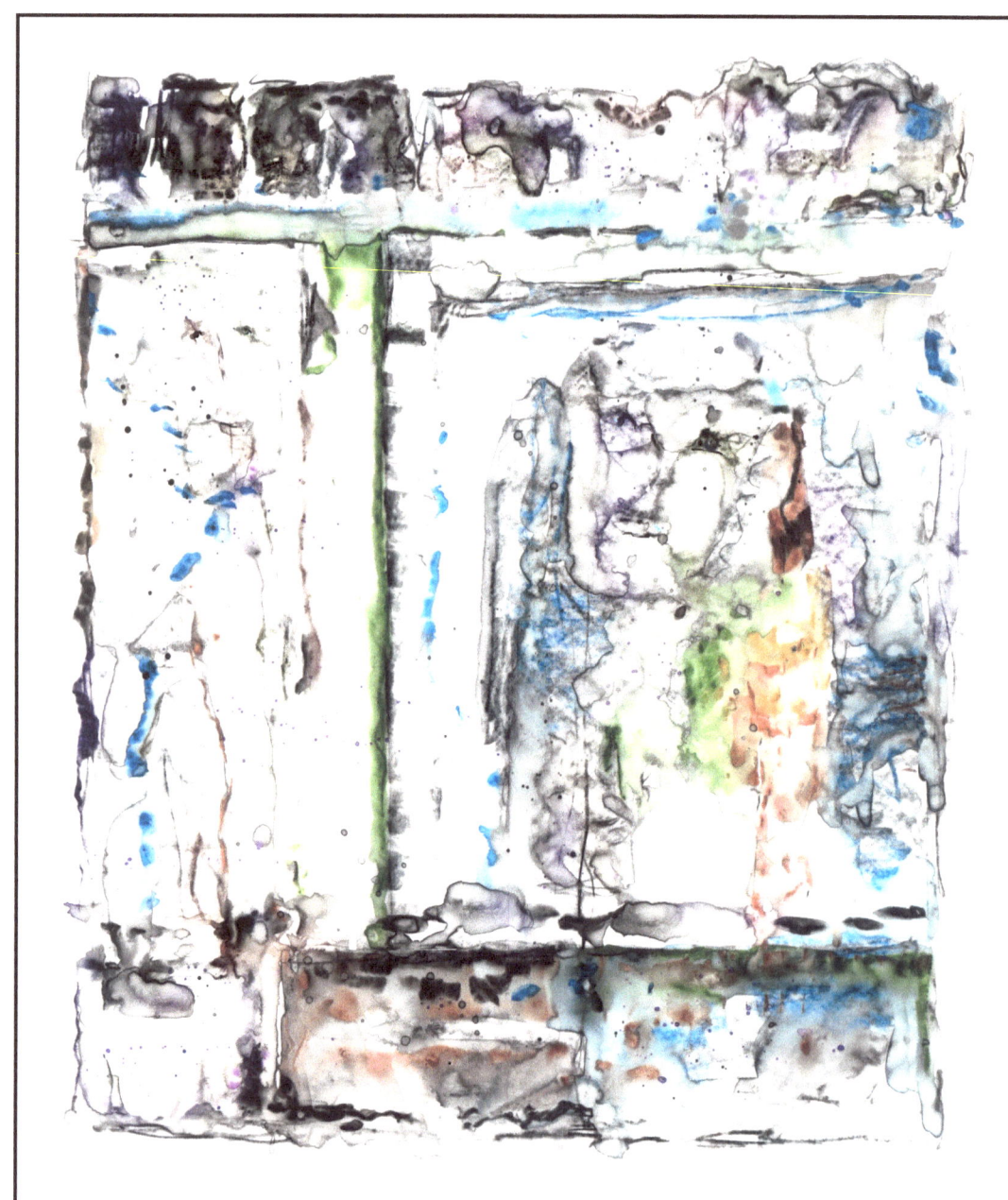

Gnomes World

"Mystery is at
the heart of
creativity. That,
and surprise."
~JULIA CAMERON

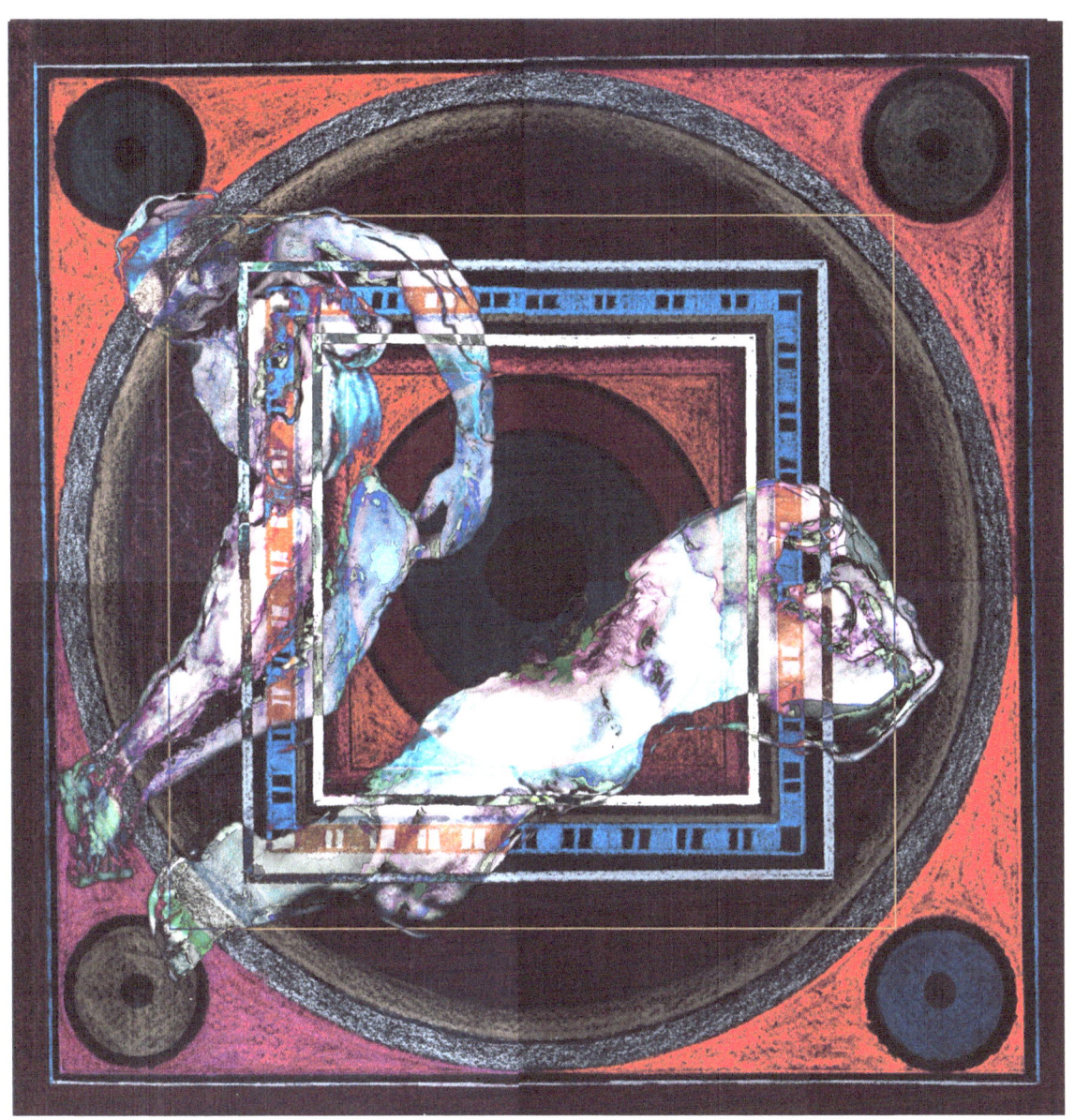

Paolo & Francesca

Paolo & Francesca fell in love but were condemned to the
first level of hell in Dante's Inferno. Francesca was
married to Paolo's older brother who killed them both.

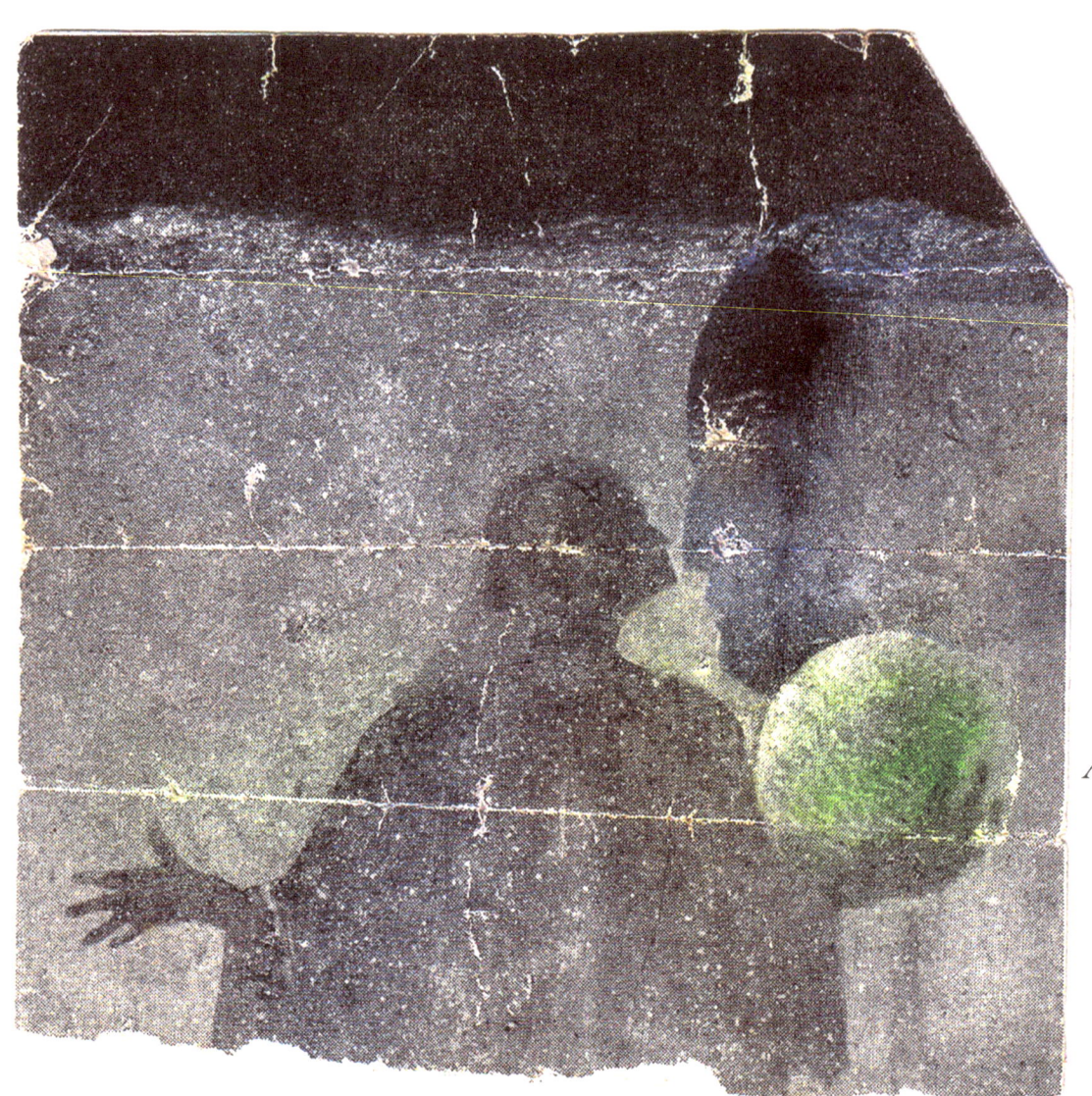

Aladdin's Wish

The metaphor of the Genie in the Lamp is the
Universe, your Higher Self, Guardian Angel or
whatever you label it. And the Genie always
says one thing: "Your wish is my command."

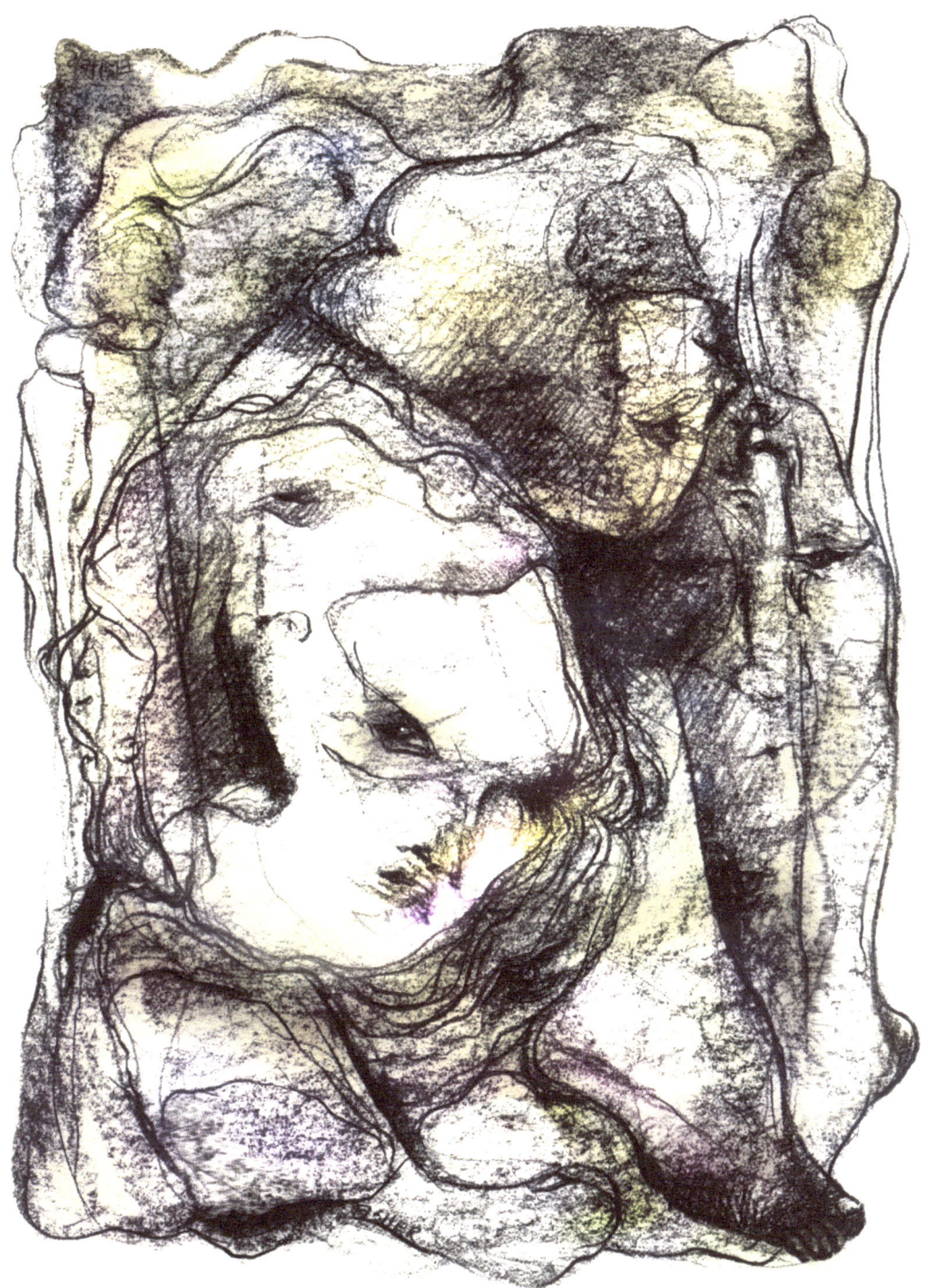

Ambivalence

Occasionally images are 'drawn forth' that can be read either up-side-down or right-side-up. It's a question which is up and which is down, right or otherwise. Rotate the image 180 degrees for an alternate view.

31

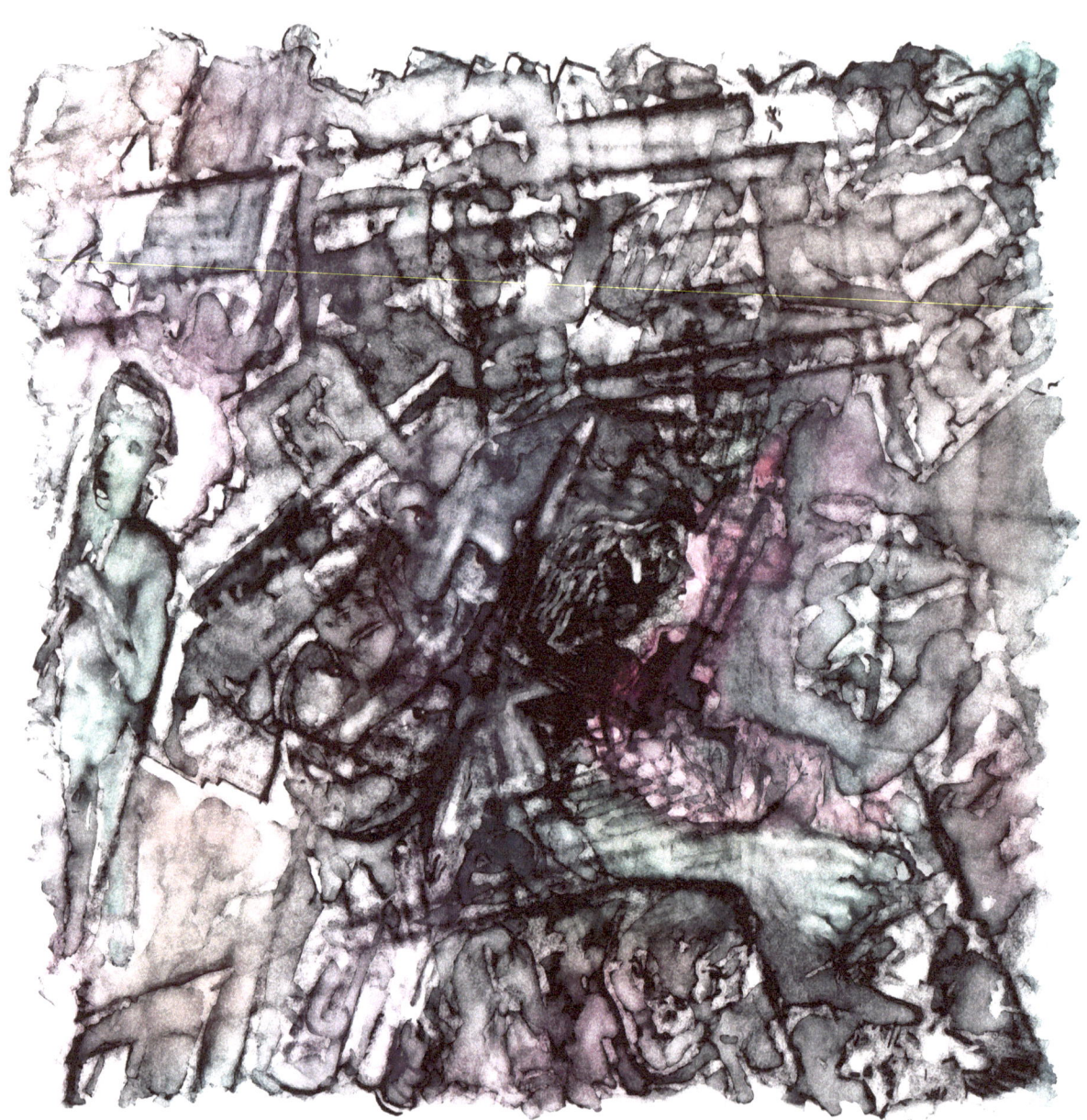

BreakUP

"The driving force, so far as it is possible for us to grasp it, seems to be in essence an urge towards self-realization." ~CARL JUNG

House of Grief

"Only in the last
moment in
history has the
delusion arisen
that people can
flourish apart
from the rest of
the living world."
~E.O. WILSON

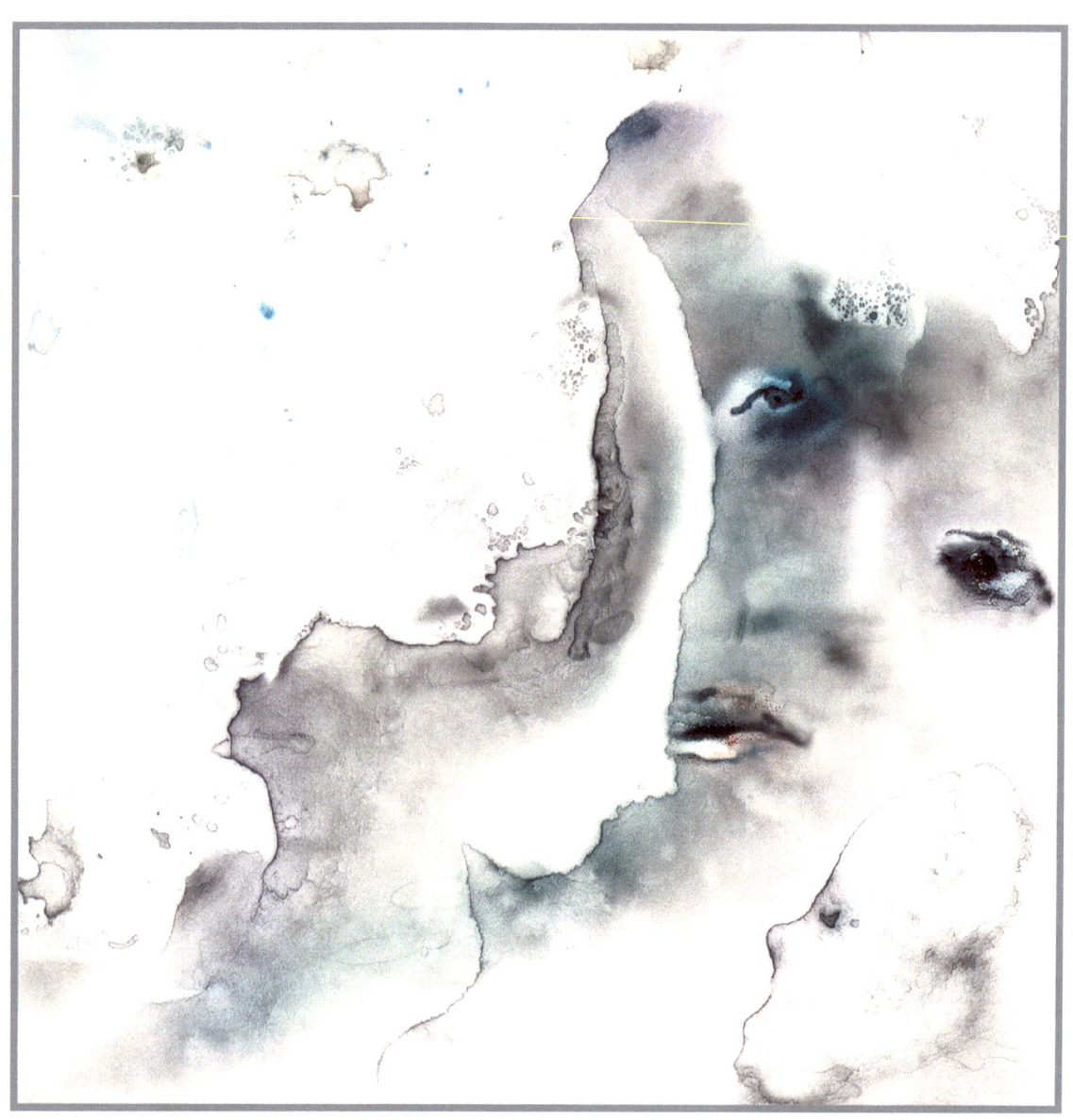

Ego Observed

"Sell your cleverness and purchase bewilderment." ~RUMI

Hell...OOO

A current manner of speech today is practiced when a one person is talking to another who is not listening: "Hell-OOO" demands attention! A call to wake up, be conscious, be in the NOW.

35

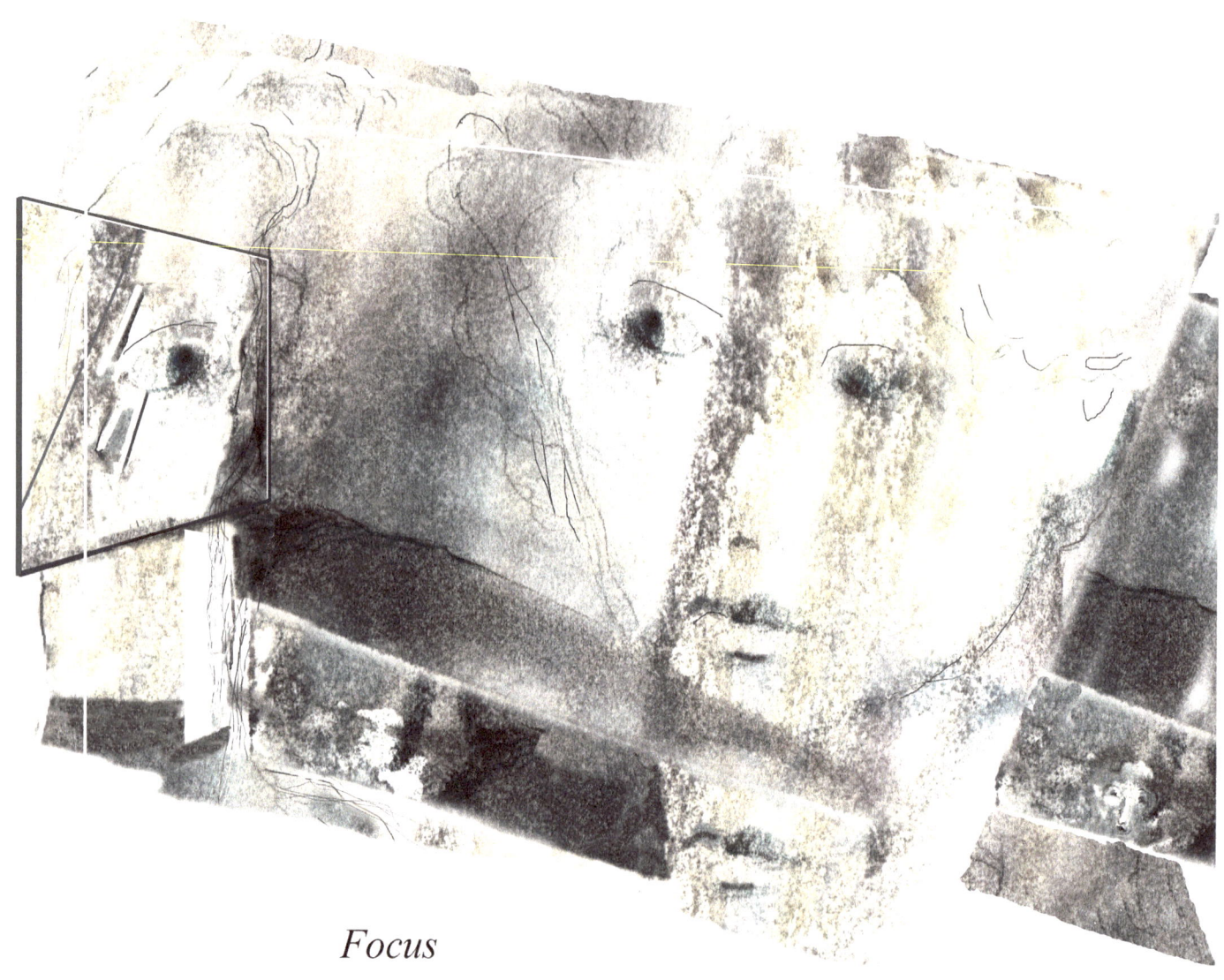

Focus

"An unknown world aspires toward reflection. Images are the oblique mirrors that hold your thoughts. You gaze into these mirror-images and catch glimpses of meaning, belonging, and shelter. Behind their bright surfaces is the dark and the silence. Images are like the god Janus, they face outward and inward at the same time."

~JOHN O'DONOHUE, *Anam Cara, a Book of Celtic Wisdom,*1997

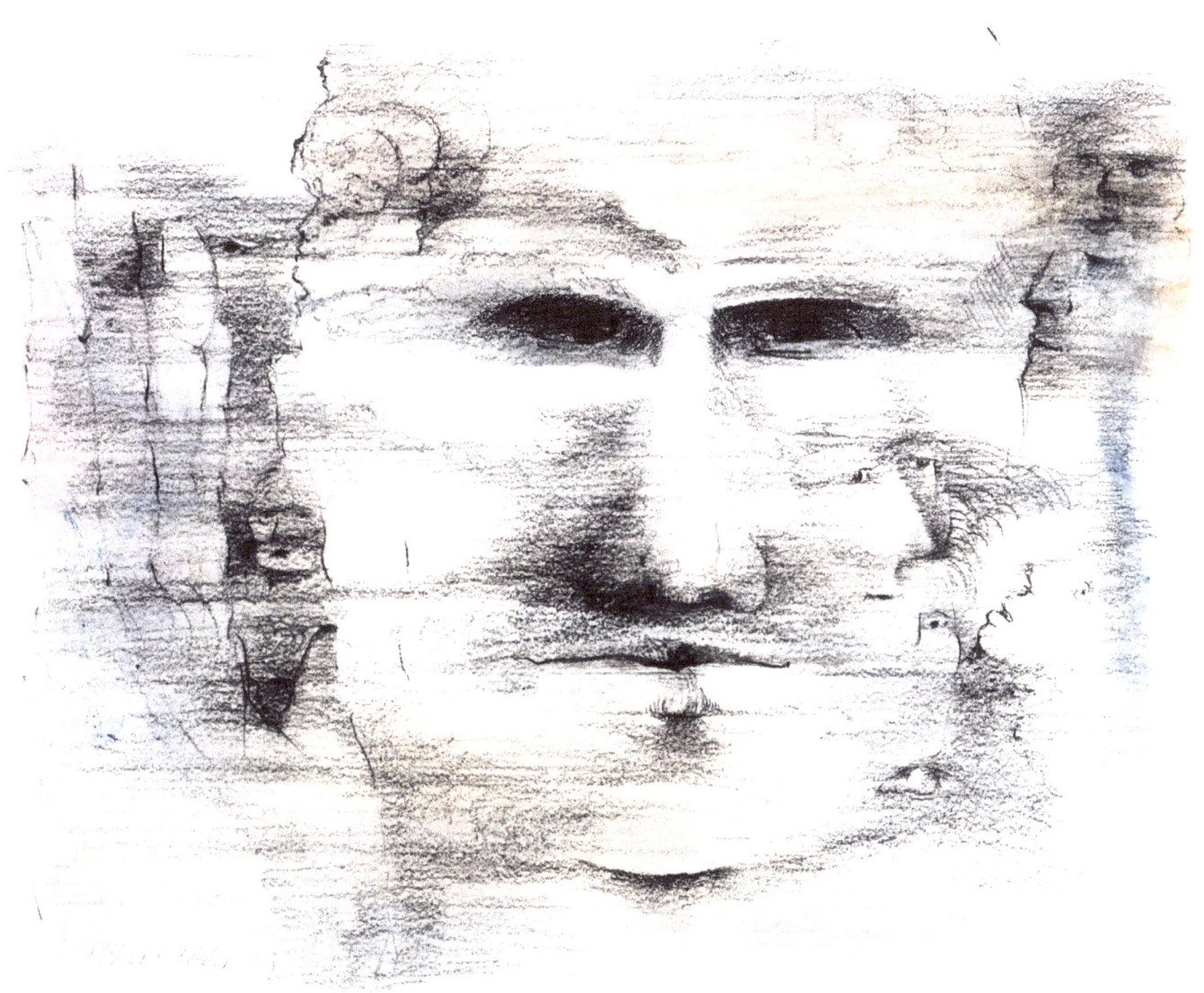

Listening

"It is strange to be here. The mystery never leaves you alone. Behind your image, below your words, above your thoughts, the silence of another world waits."

~JOHN O'DONOHUE, *Anam Cara, A Book of Celtic Wisdom,*1997

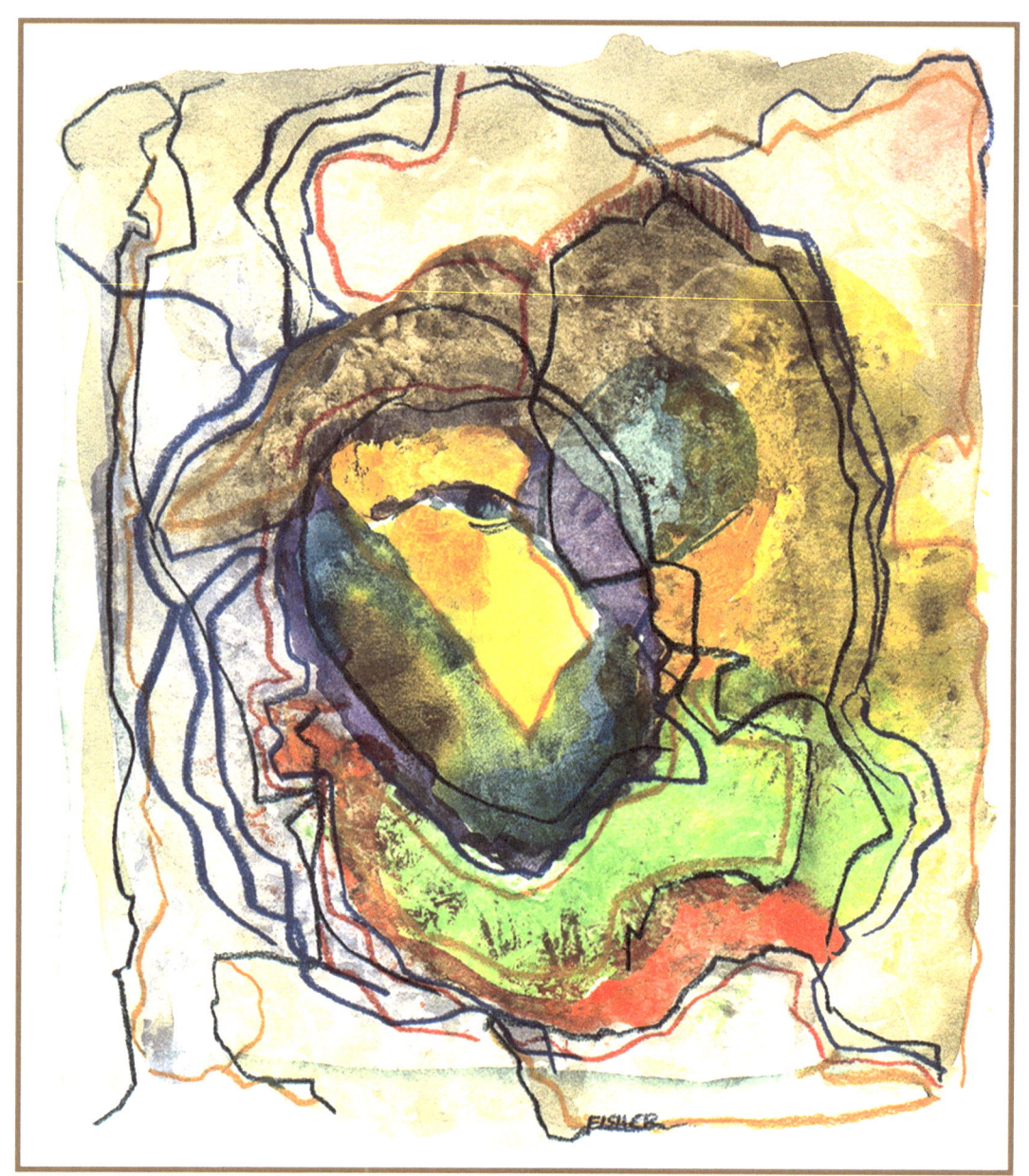

Egoist

Artworks are meant to reveal the sacred;
they are portals to full consciousness.

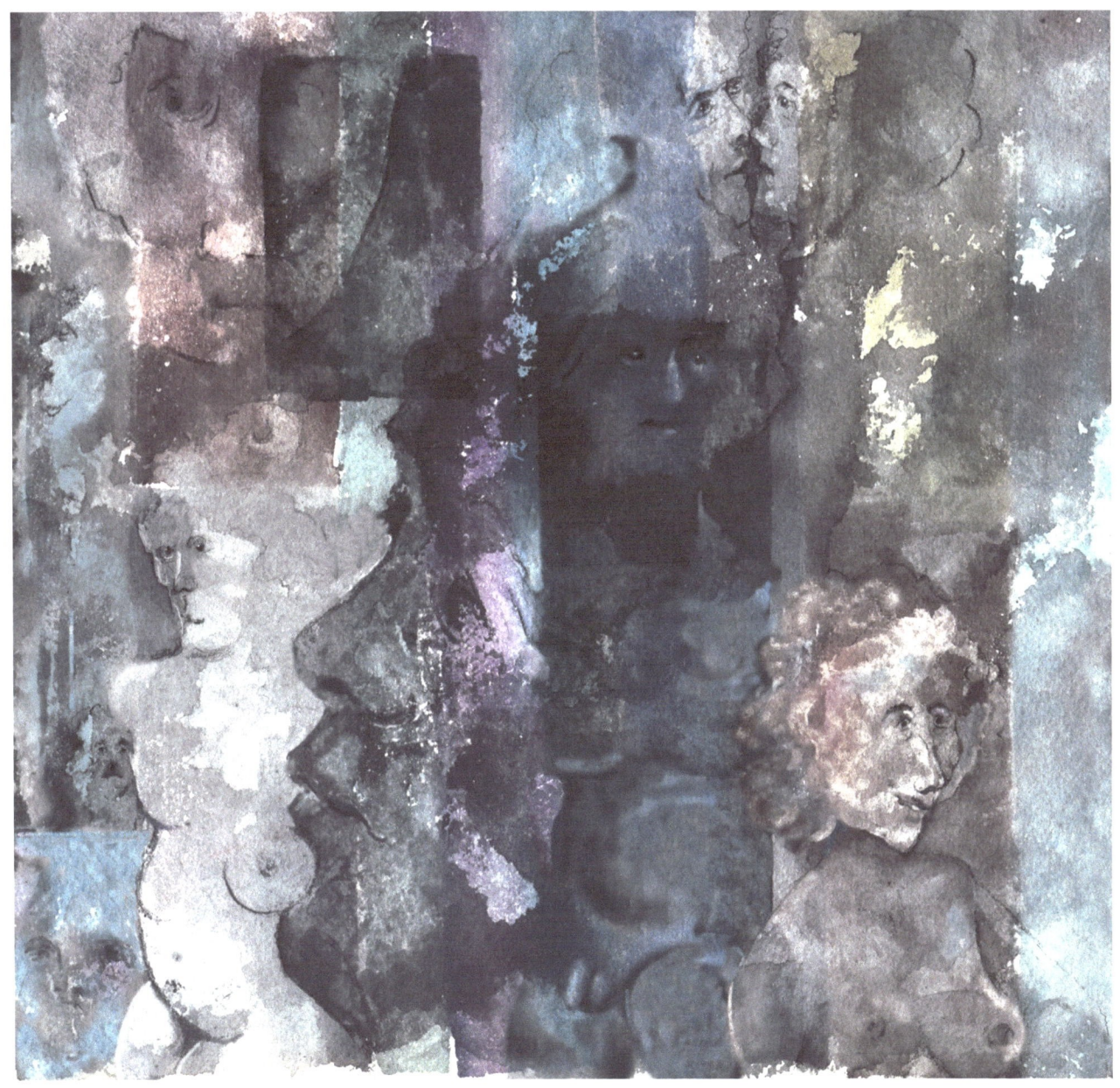

Blue Funk

"What lies behind us and what lies before us
are tiny matters compared to what lies within us."
~RALPH WALDO EMERSON

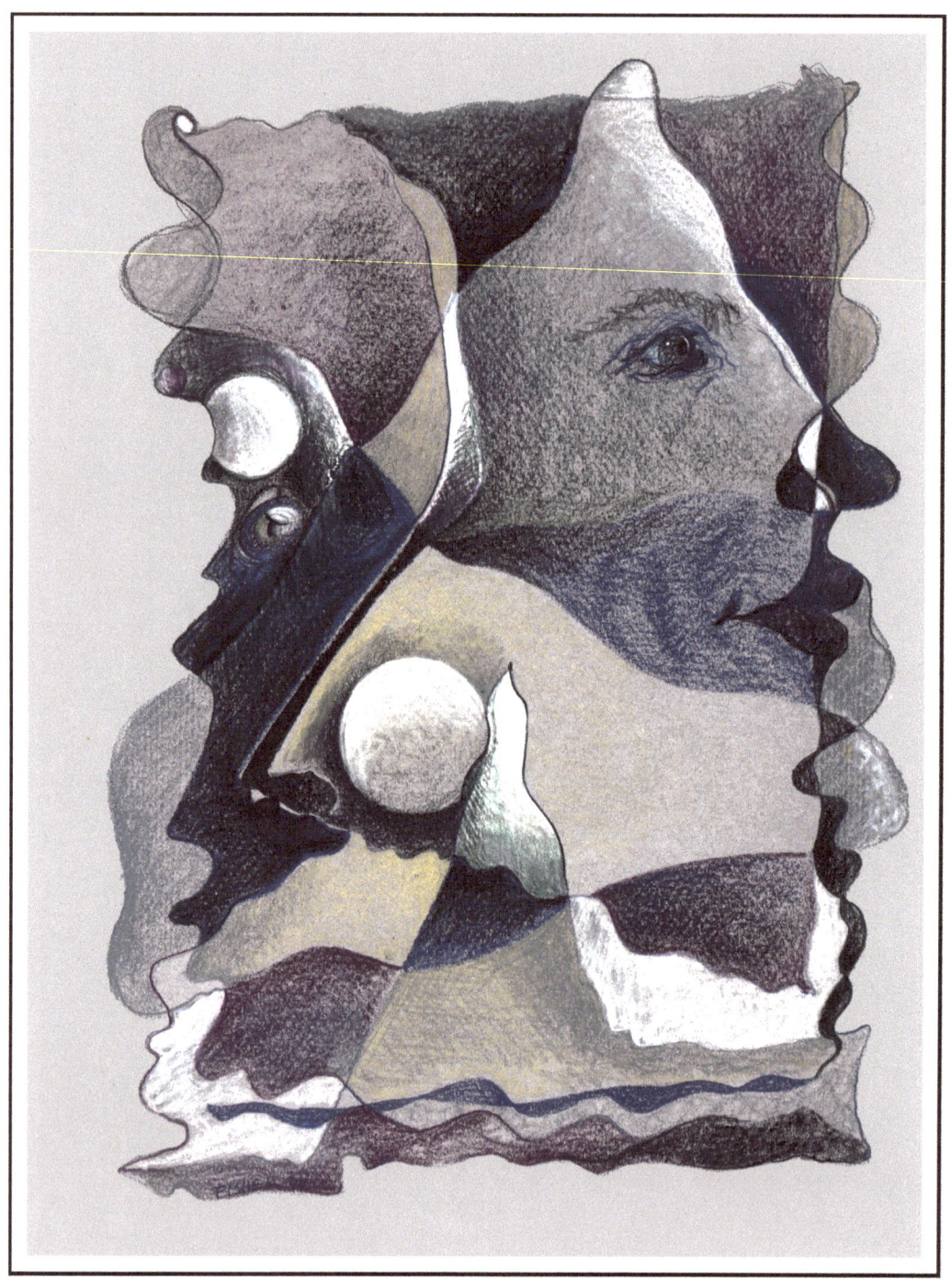

The Fool

"Ego is always
identifcation with
form...seeking
yourself in some
form, especially
thought forms,
energy forms...
the voice in your
head that never
stops speaking."
~ECKHART TOLLE
A New Earth, 2005

40

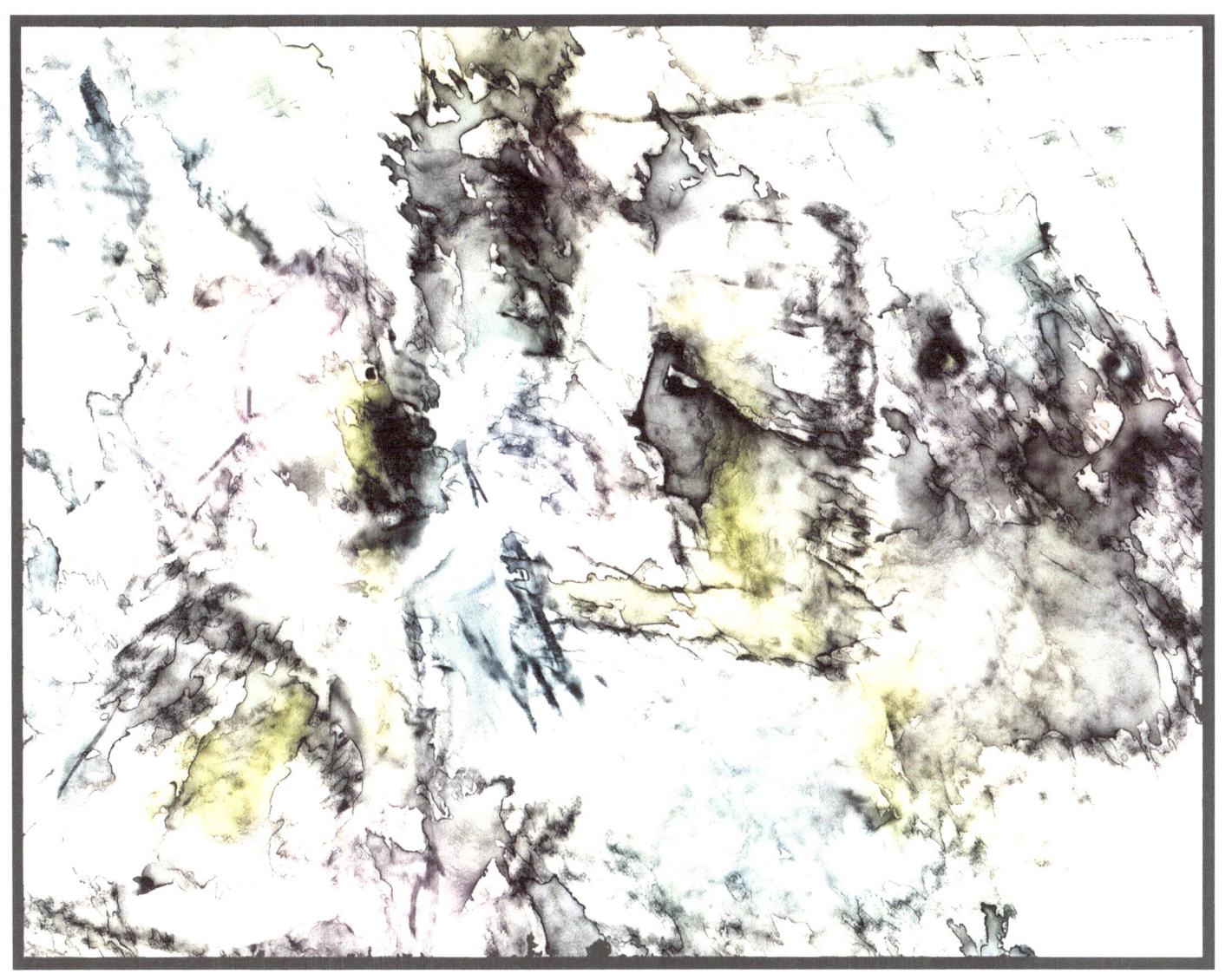

I'm Right, You're Wrong

"It is only when we have renounced our pre-occupation with 'I,' 'me,' 'mine' that we can truly possess the world in which we live. Everything is ours, pro-vided that we regard nothing as our property. And not only is everything ours; it is also everybody else's." ~ALDOUS HUXLEY, *The Perennial Philosophy, 1944*

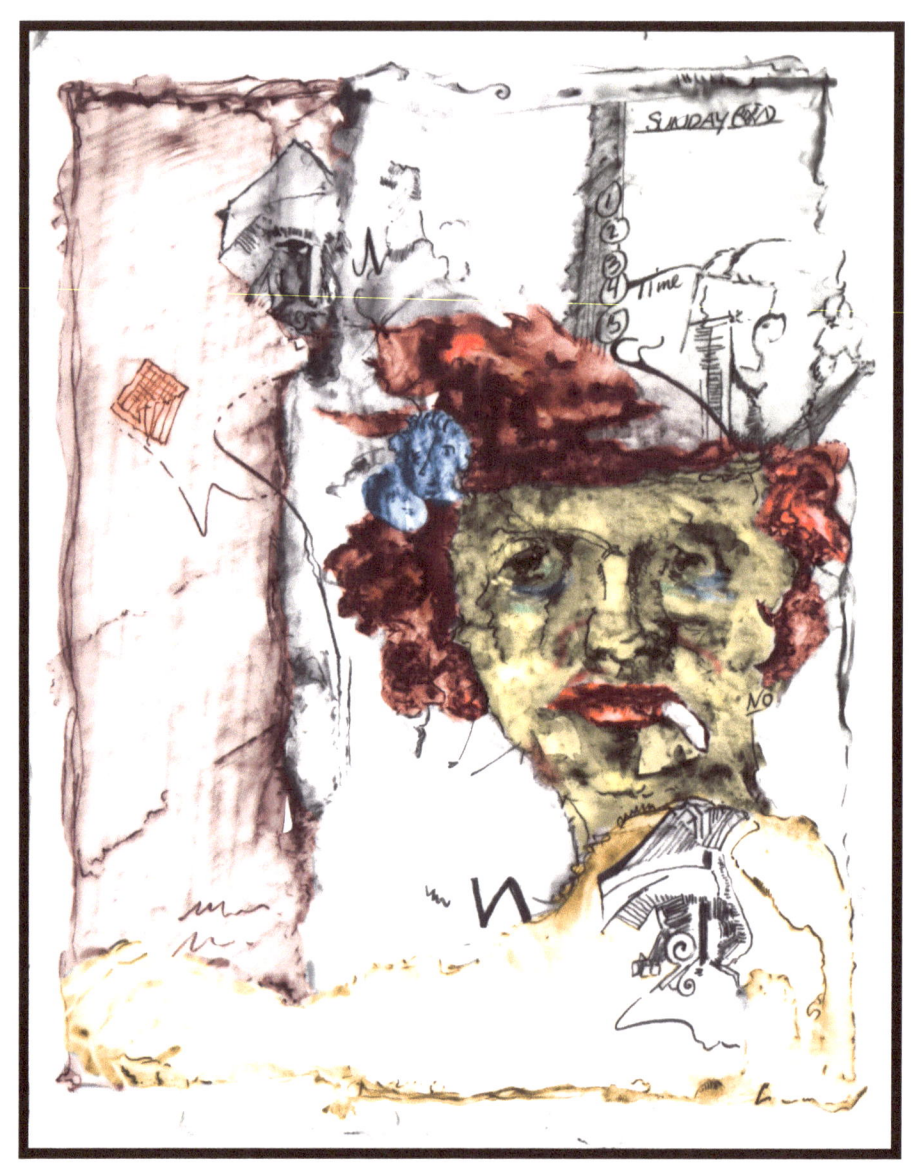

Whatever Lola Wants, Lola Gets

This image came forth during a time of anger.
The following Sunday the NY Times had a
Matisse work which could be her close cousin.

Mangled Togetherness

"...by means of drawing, we can unlock a door not otherwise open to consciousness."
~BETTY EDWARDS, *Drawing on the Right Side of the Brain. 1979*

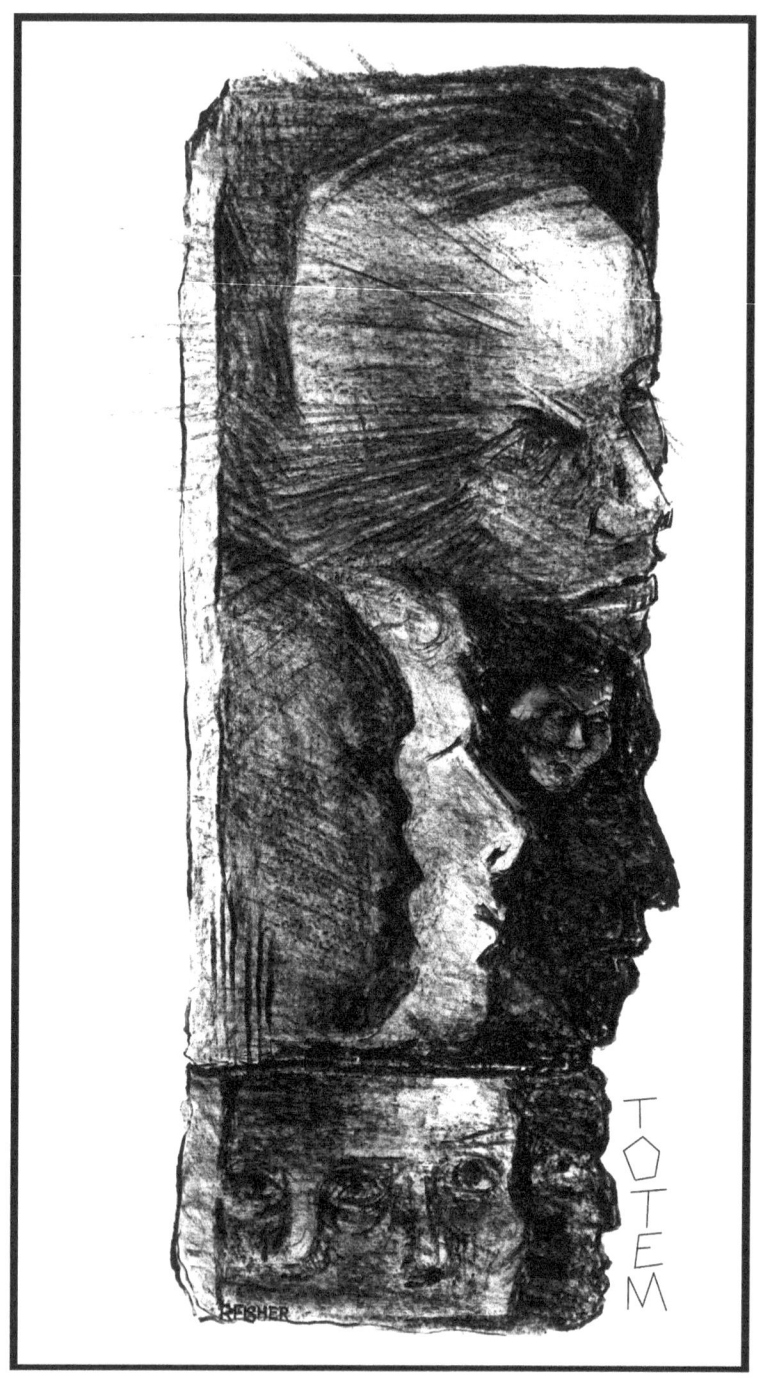

Totem

"In the human face, the anonymity of the universe becomes intimate. The human face is the icon of creation."
~JOHN O'DONOHUE, *Anam Cara, a Book of Celtic Wisdom*, 1997

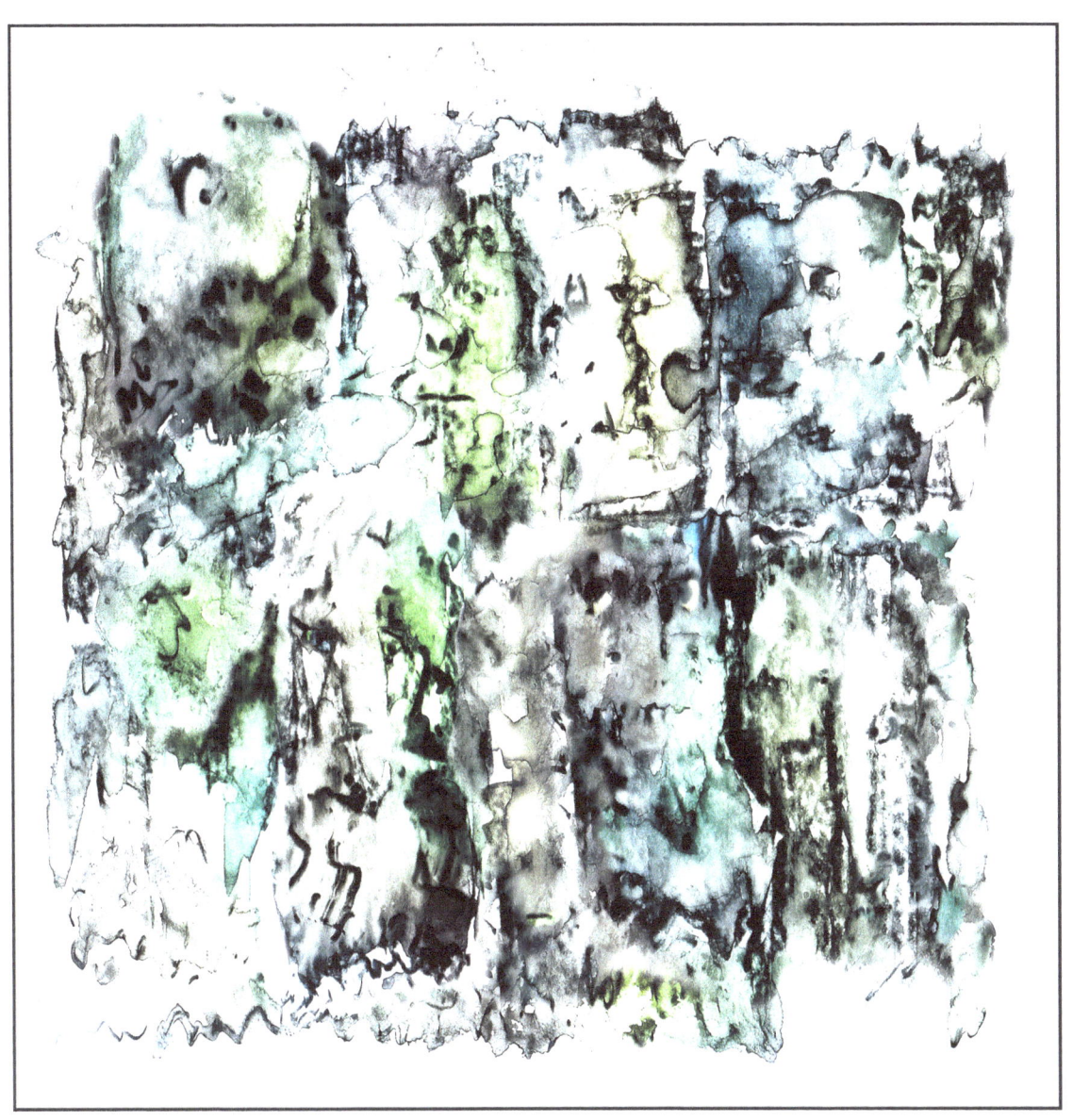

Silent Friends

Silence hold secrets. The sweetest sound is the
sound of stillness, the song of the soul.

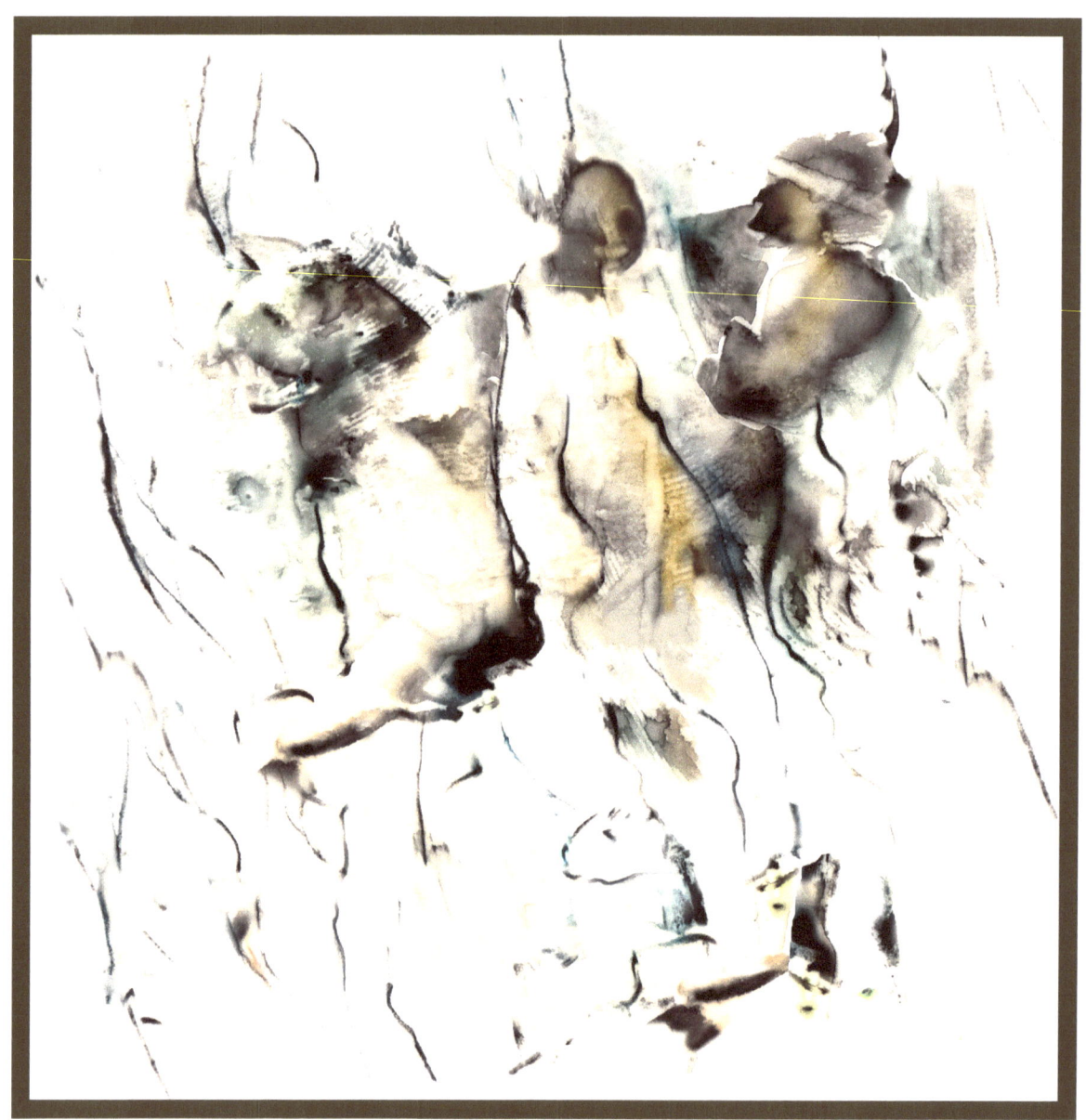

Two Figures and a Beast

"Je ne cherche pas, je trouve.
I do not search, I find."
~PABLO PICASSO

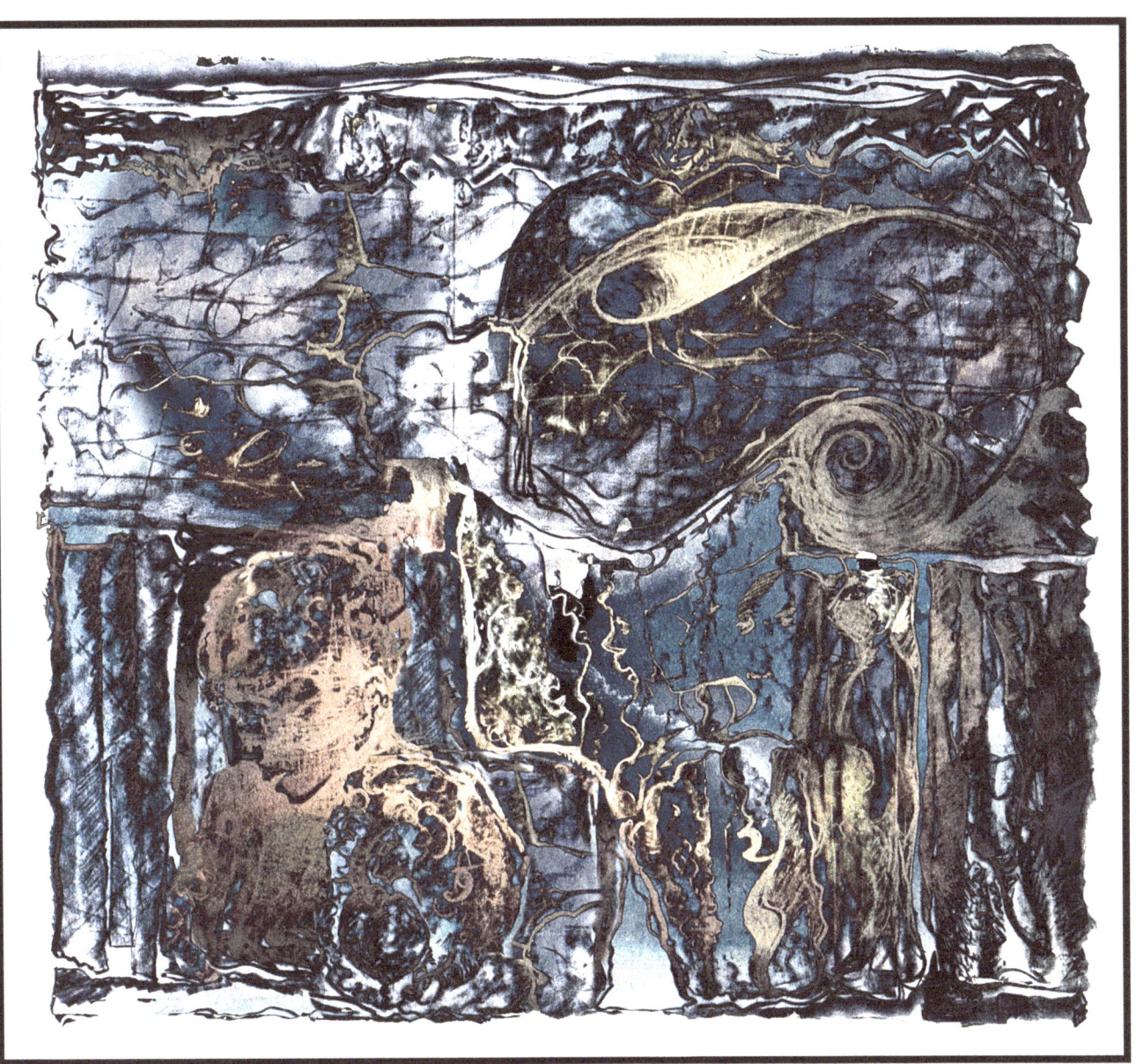

Malaise

"We are seldom in the place where we stand and in the time that is now. Few people are actually able to inhabit their present time because they are too stressed and rushed."
~JOHN O'DONOHUE, *Anam Cara, a Book of Celtic Wisdom, 1997*

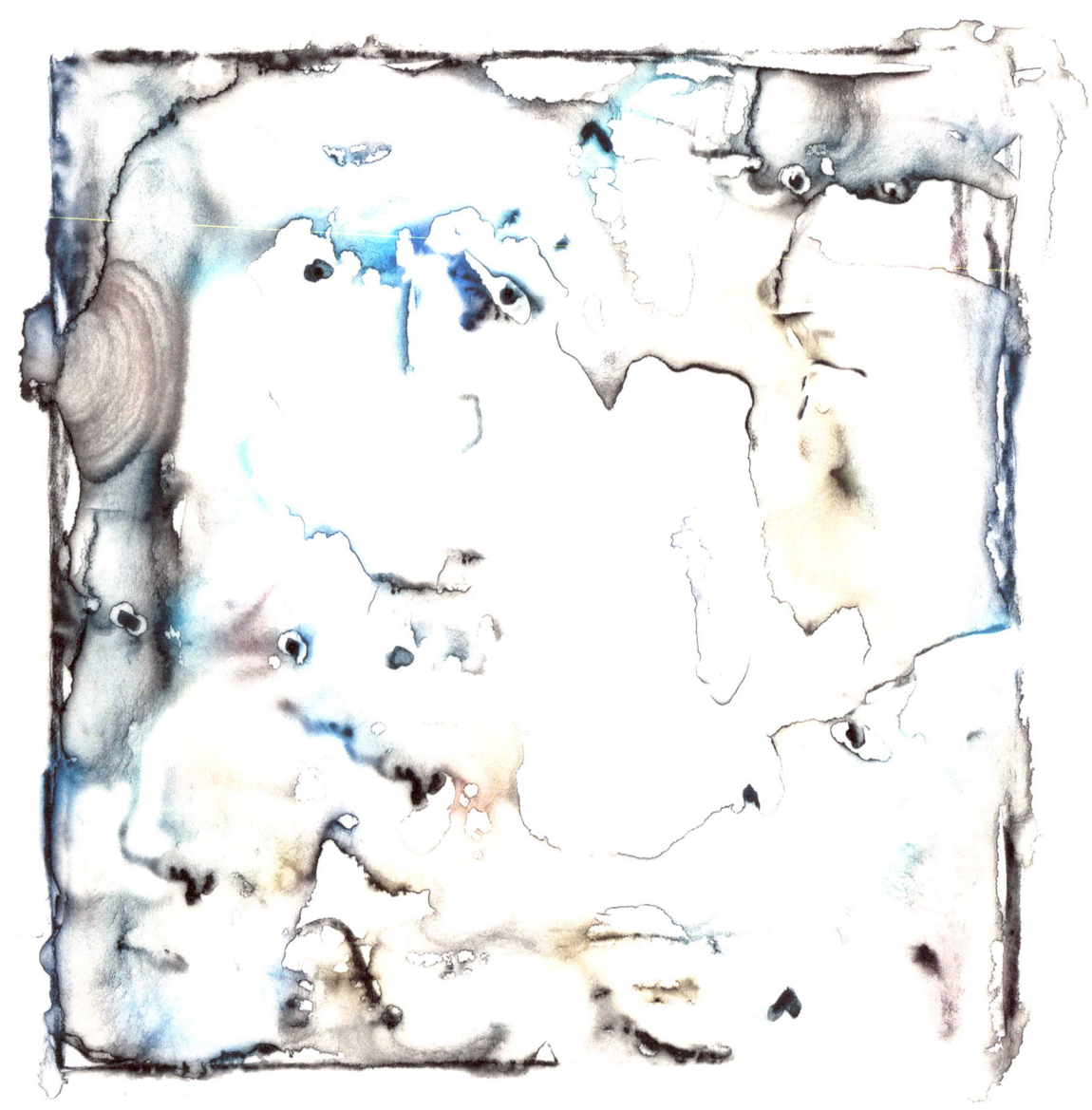

What I Think Others Think

"Truth has an elegance that startles
the heart to its own reawakening."
~NEALE DONALD WALSCH,
*Conversations With God,*1996

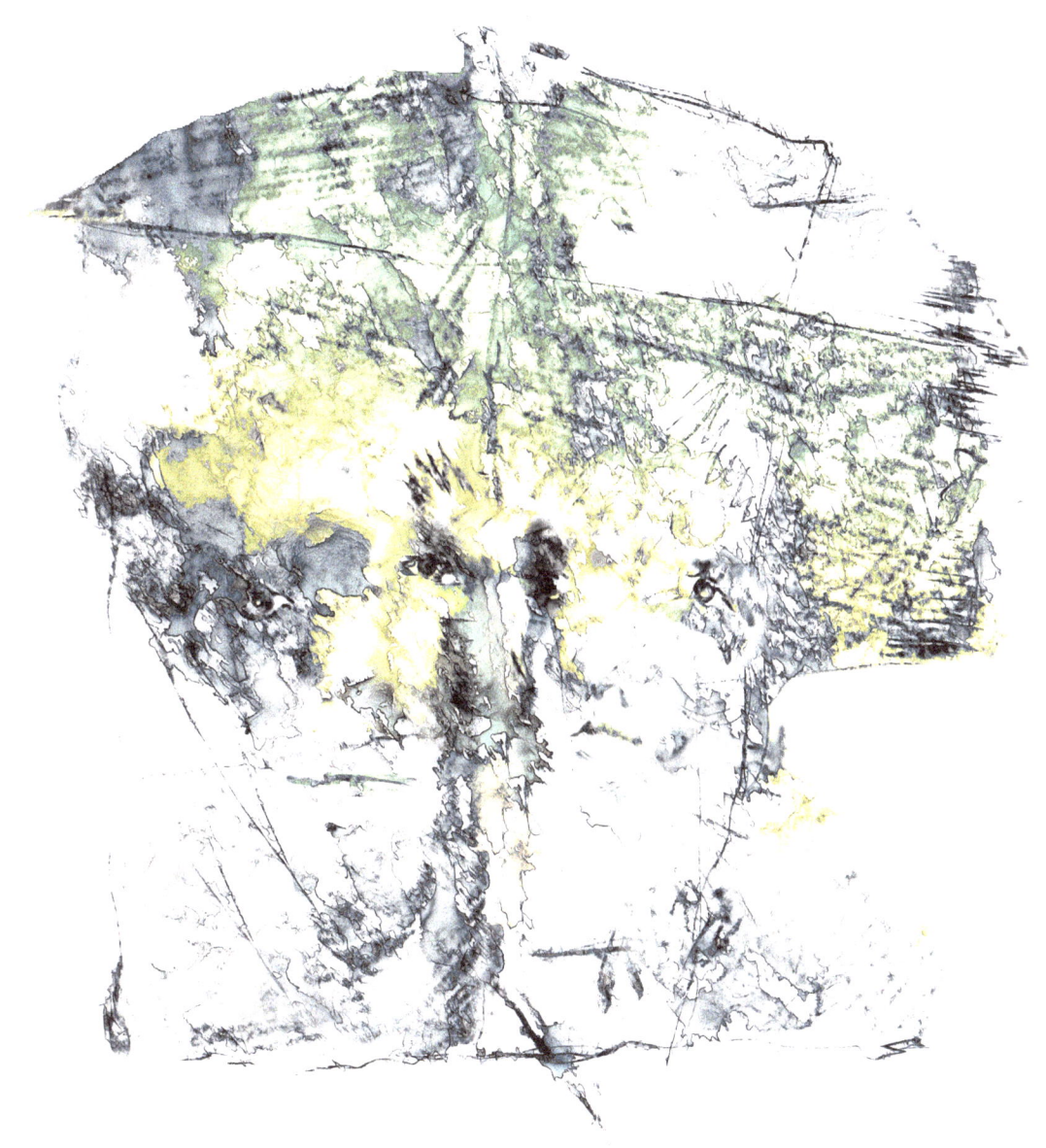

Umbrella Friends

"Although a thought only makes you think, an image
touches and affects our whole being."
~HENRY REED, *Edgar Cayce on Channeling Your Higher Self*, 1989

49

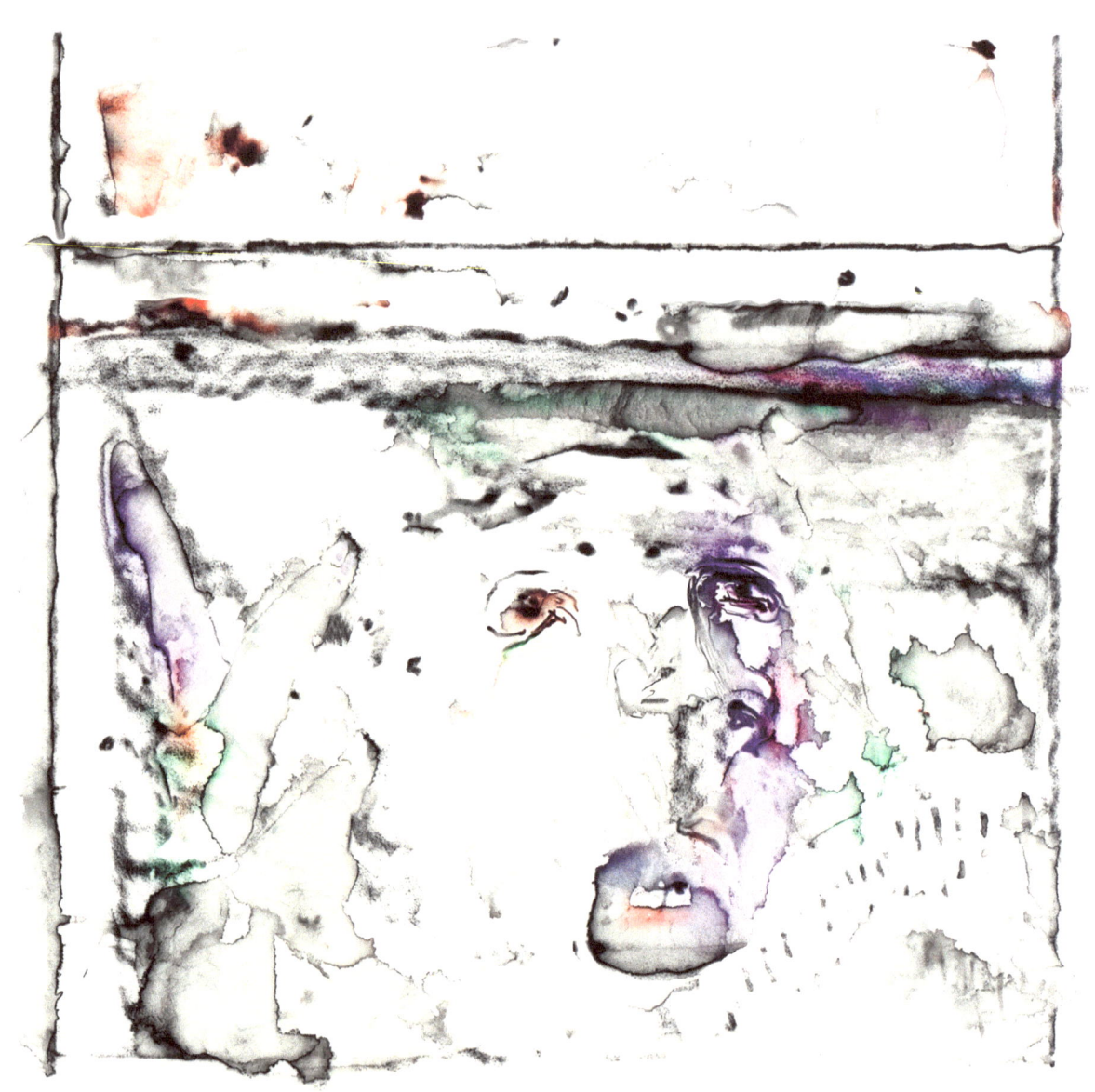

Trapped in Thought

"If the doors of perception were cleansed everything would appear to man as it is, infinite." ~WILLIAM BLAKE

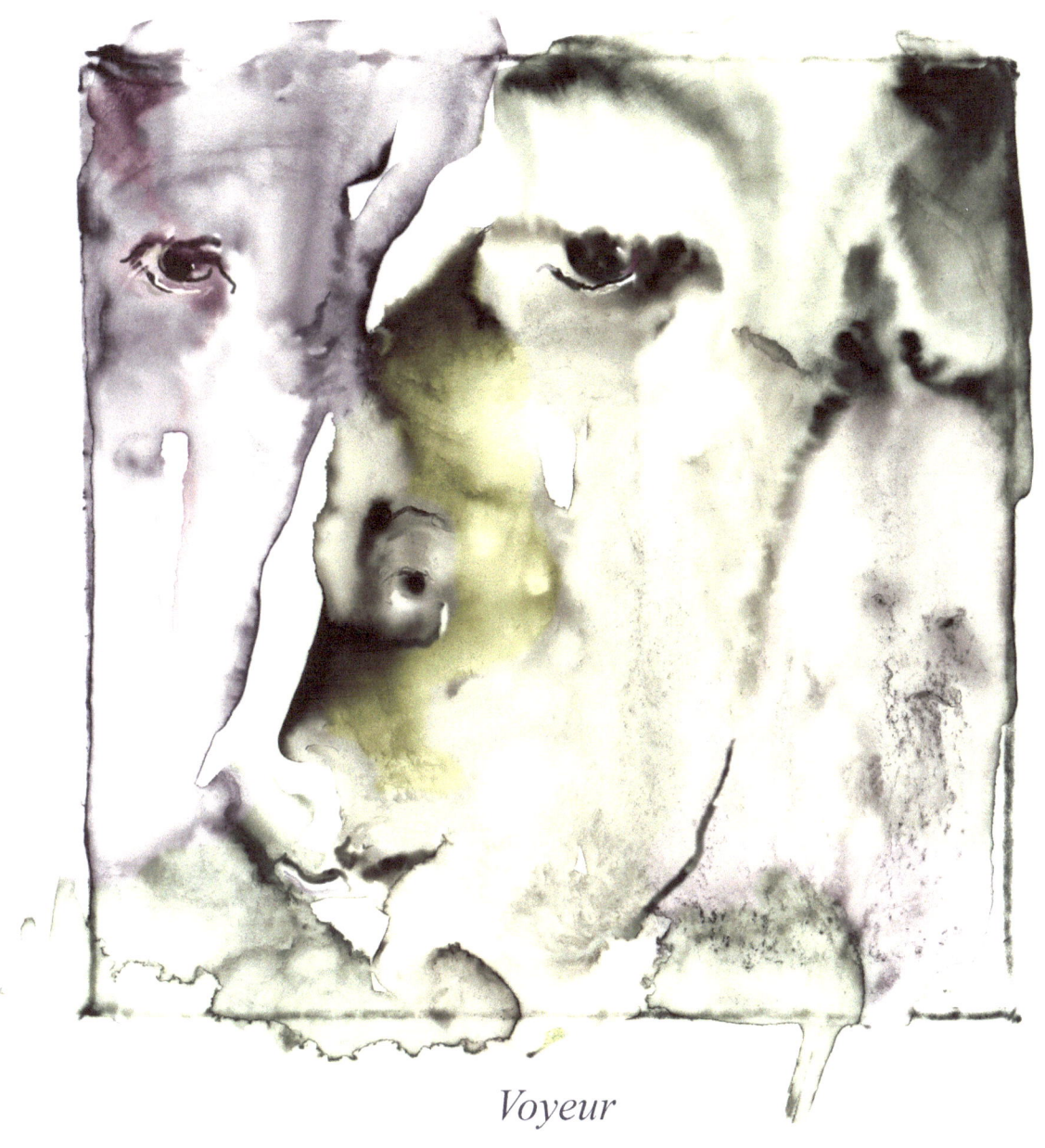

Voyeur

"Consume my heart away; sick with desire
And fastened to a dying animal" ~YEATS

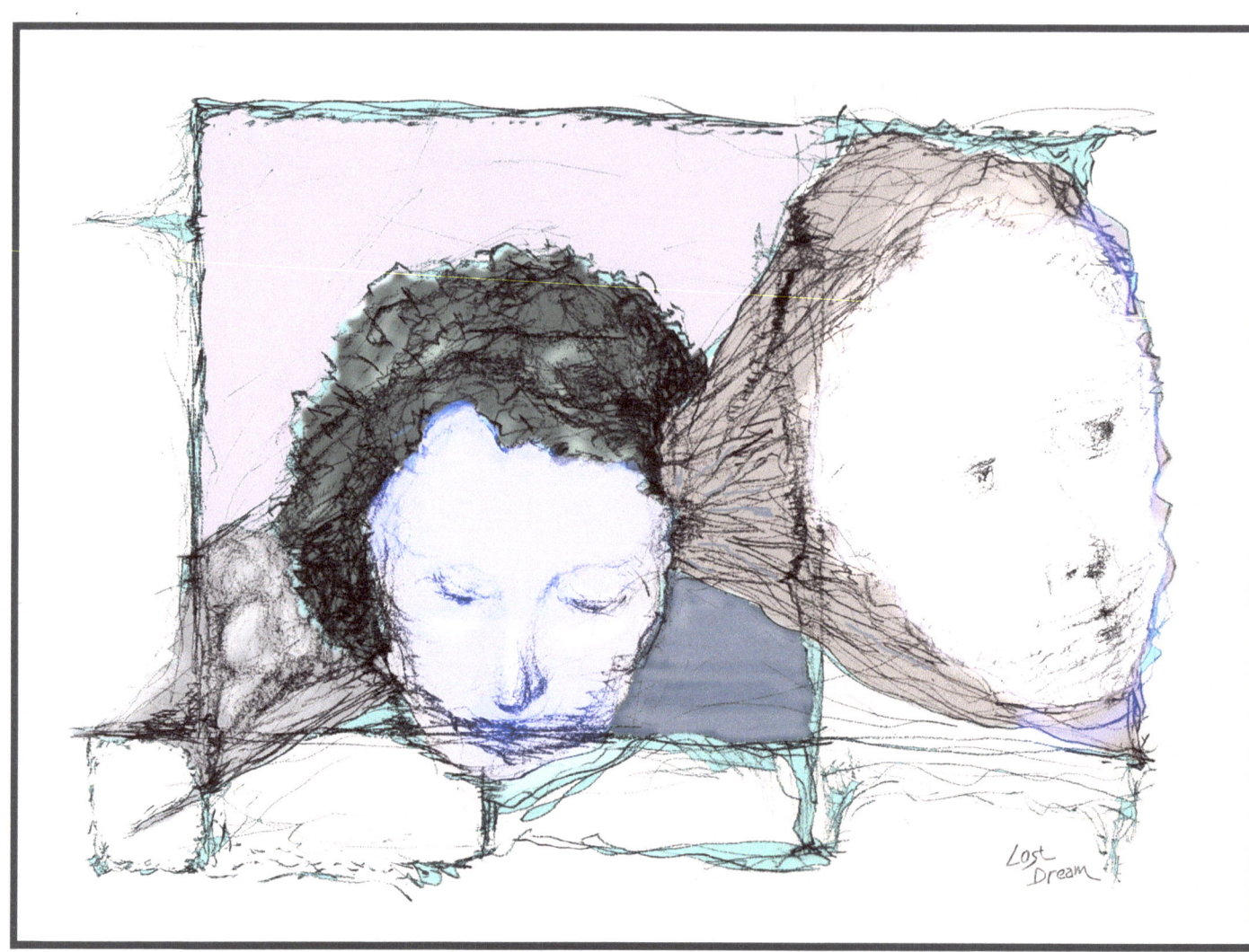

Lost Dream

"I think that maybe I will be a little surer of being a little nearer. That's all. Eternity is in the understanding that--that little is more than enough."

~R.S.THOMAS

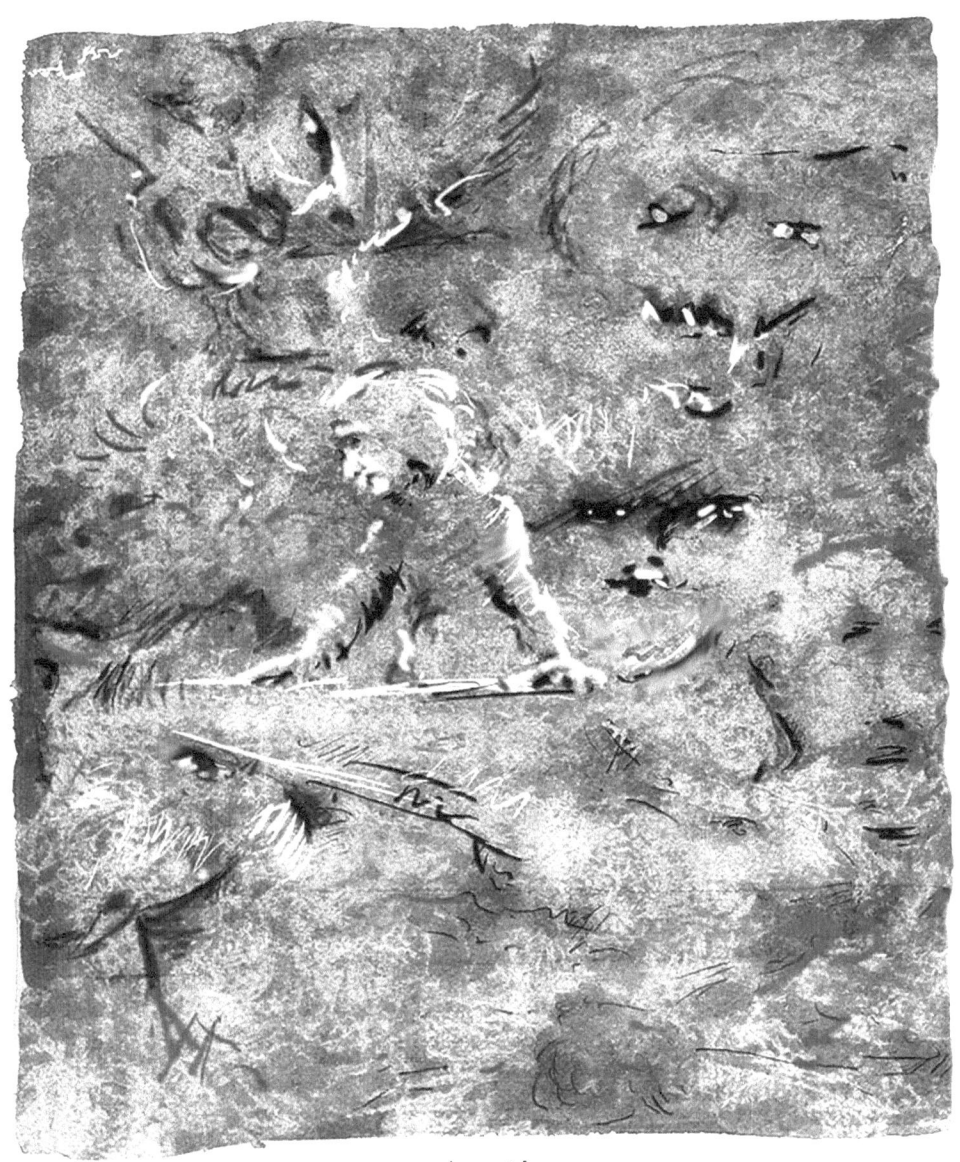

Anvil

Mankind probably cannot survive much longer unless there is a profound shift of consciousness within the human race. The dysfunction of the human mind is becoming intolerant to the planet. With the aid of new technologies people are killing each other more efficiently and at an increasingly alarming rate.

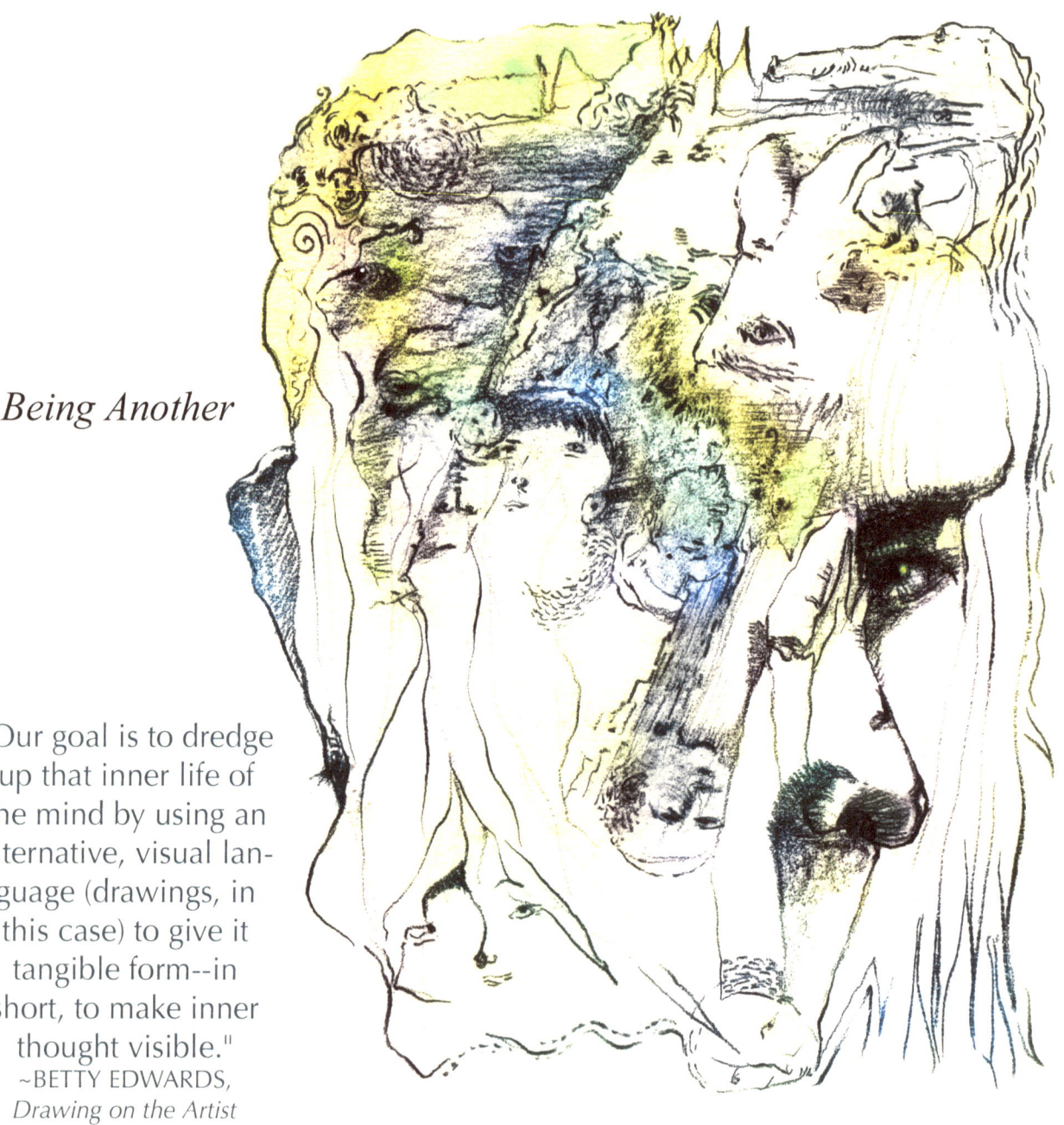

Being Another

"Our goal is to dredge up that inner life of the mind by using an alternative, visual language (drawings, in this case) to give it tangible form--in short, to make inner thought visible."
~BETTY EDWARDS,
Drawing on the Artist Within, 1986

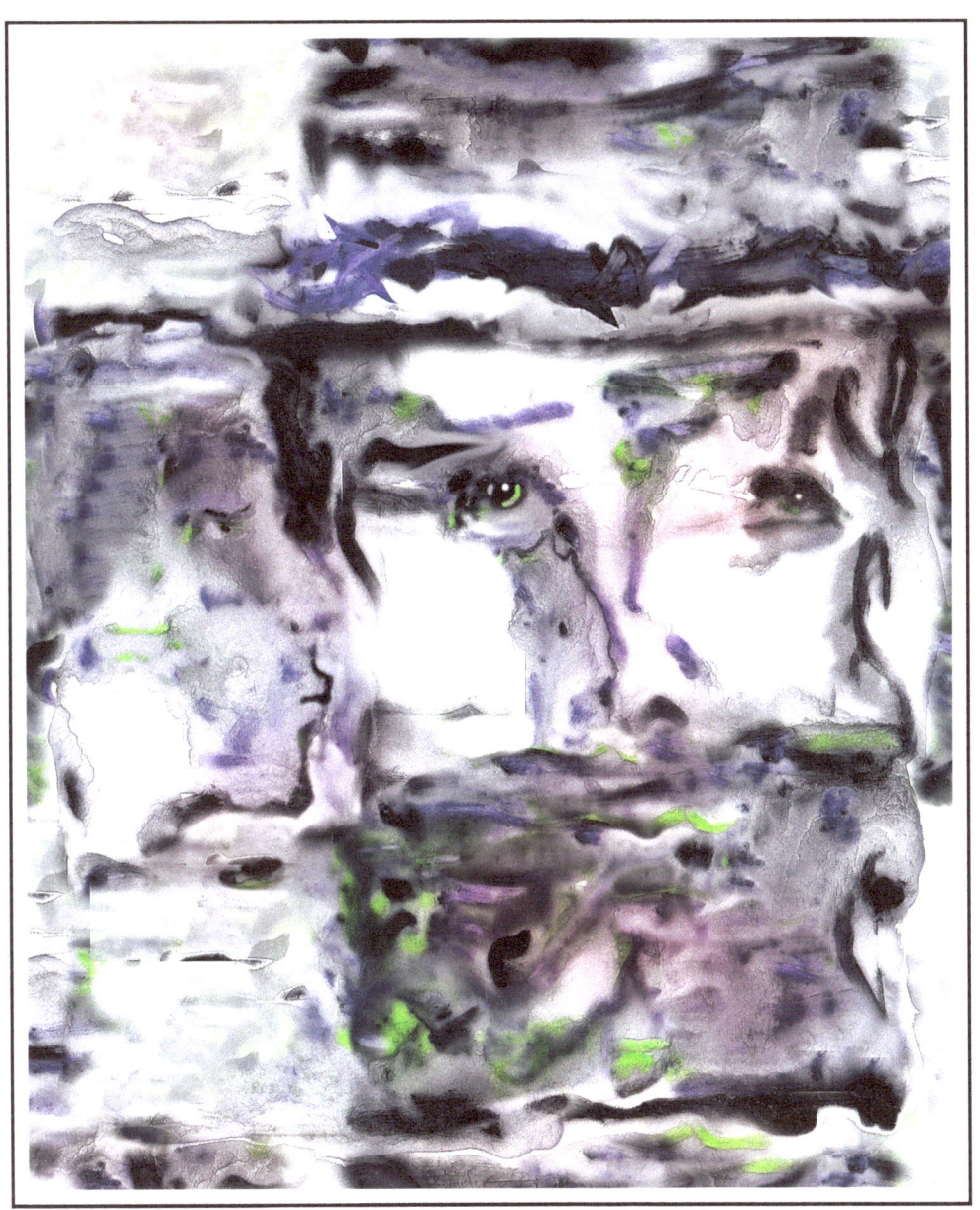

Thornes

"Suffering cracks open the shell of ego, and then comes a point when it has served its purpose. Suffering is necessary until you realize it is unnecessary." ~ECKHART TOLLE, *Stillness Speaks*, 2003

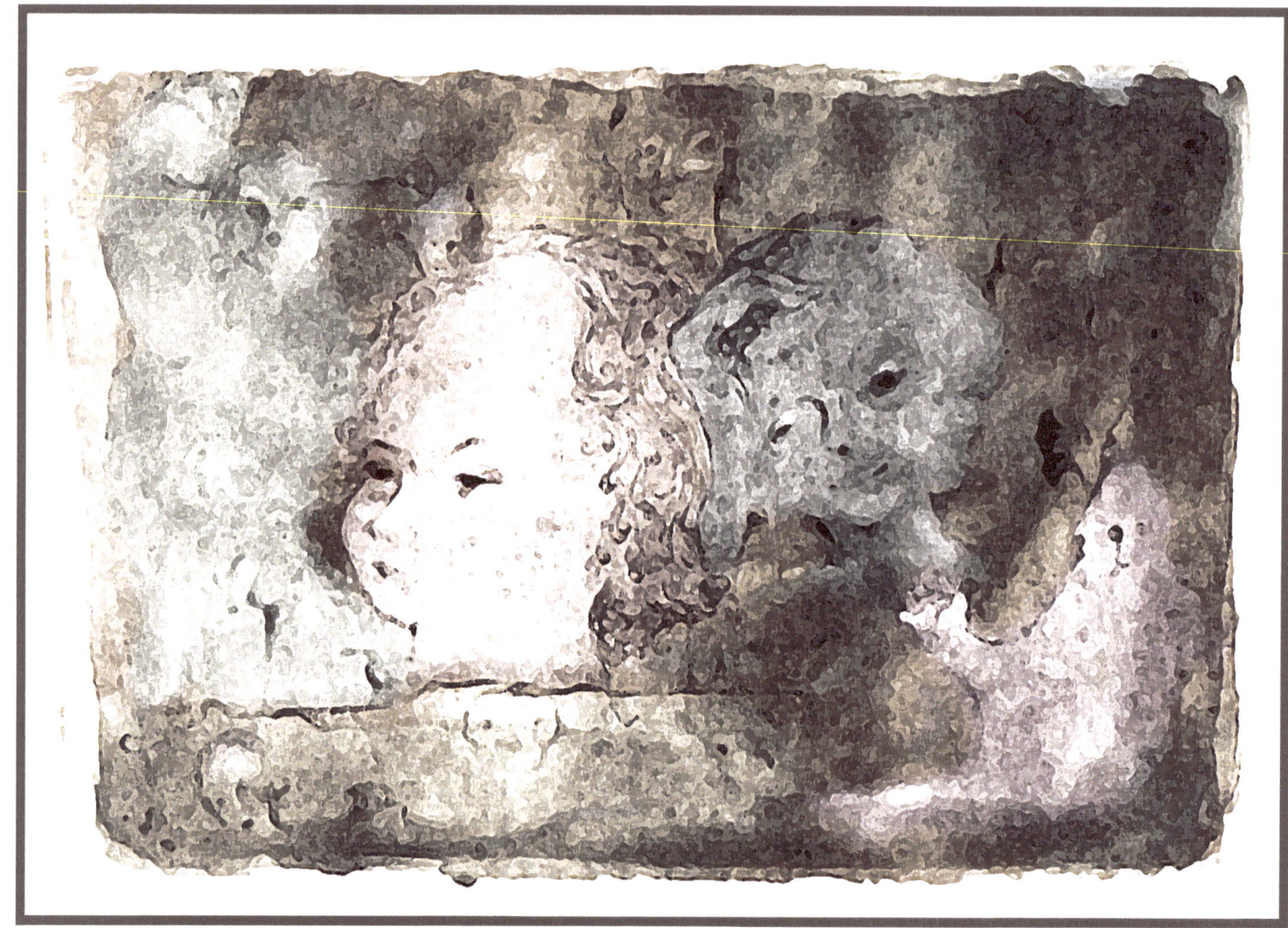

Generations

"Who made this night?
A forge deep in the earth-mud.
What is the body? Endurance.
What is love? Gratitude.
What is hidden in our chests? Laughter.
What else? Compassion." ~RUMI

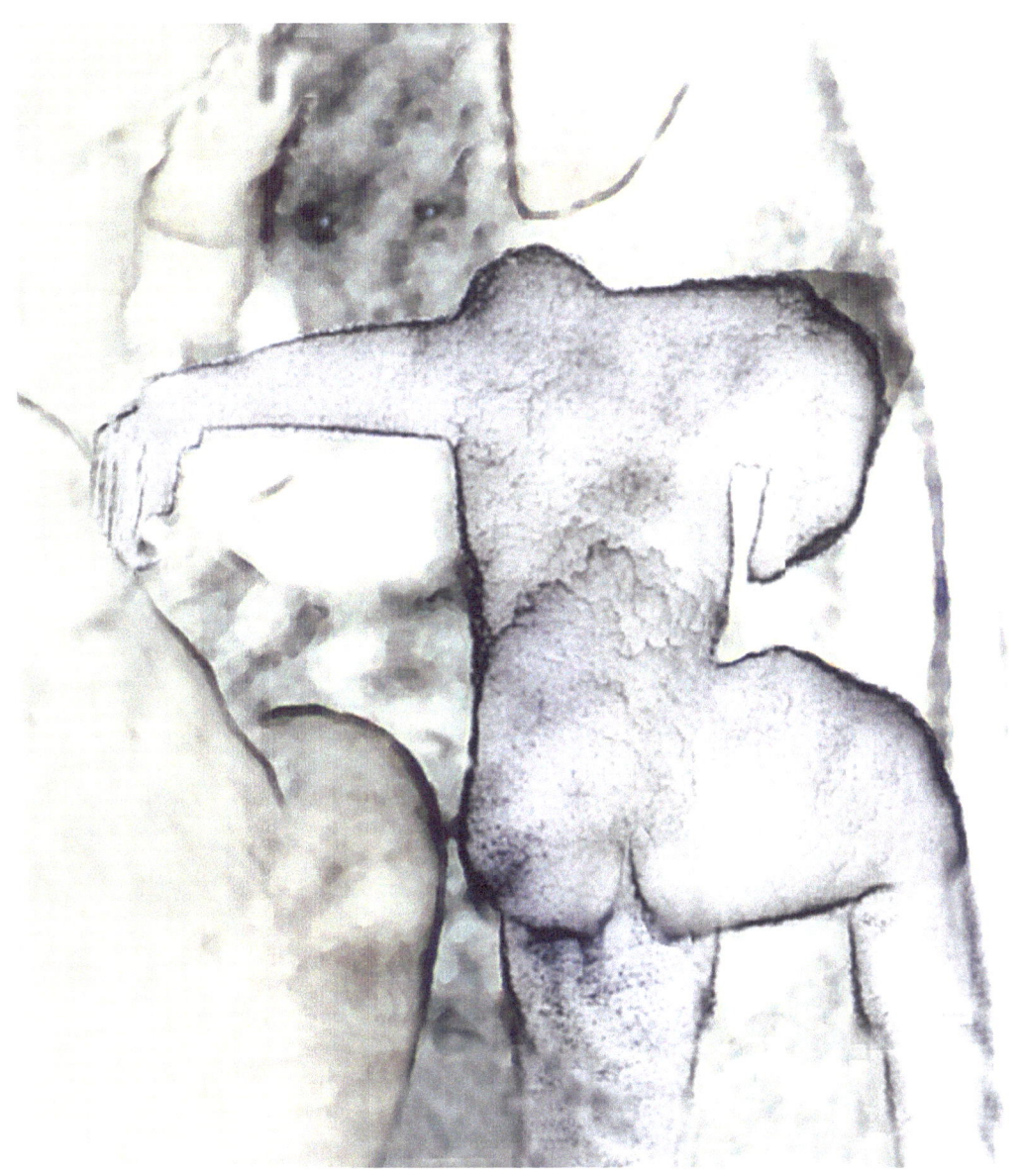

Torso 2

"All important things in art have always originated from the deepest feeling about the mystery of Being." ~MAX BECKMANN

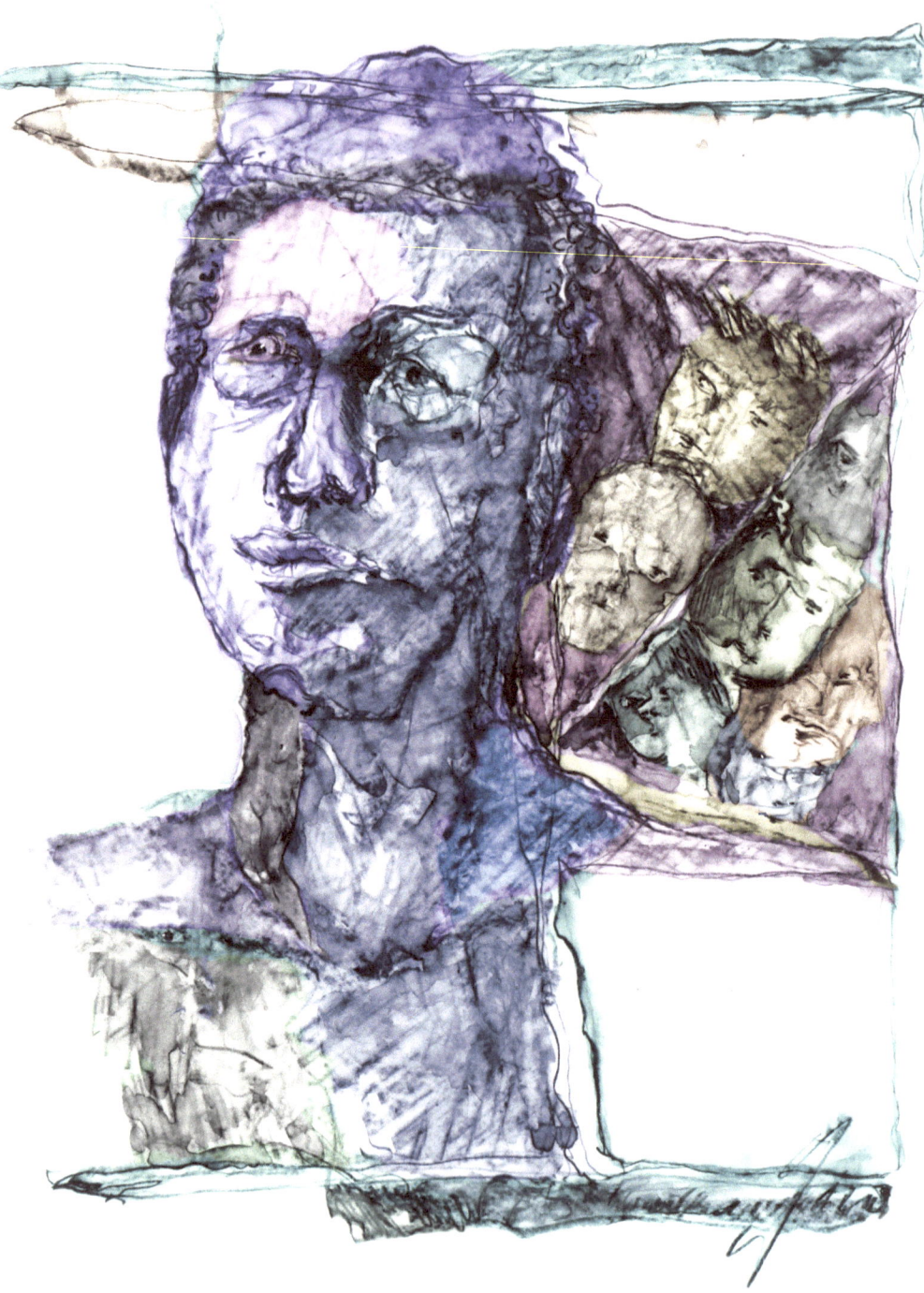

On My Mind

"Spirituality is
my work.
The two are
inseparable."
~DAVID
ELLSWORTH

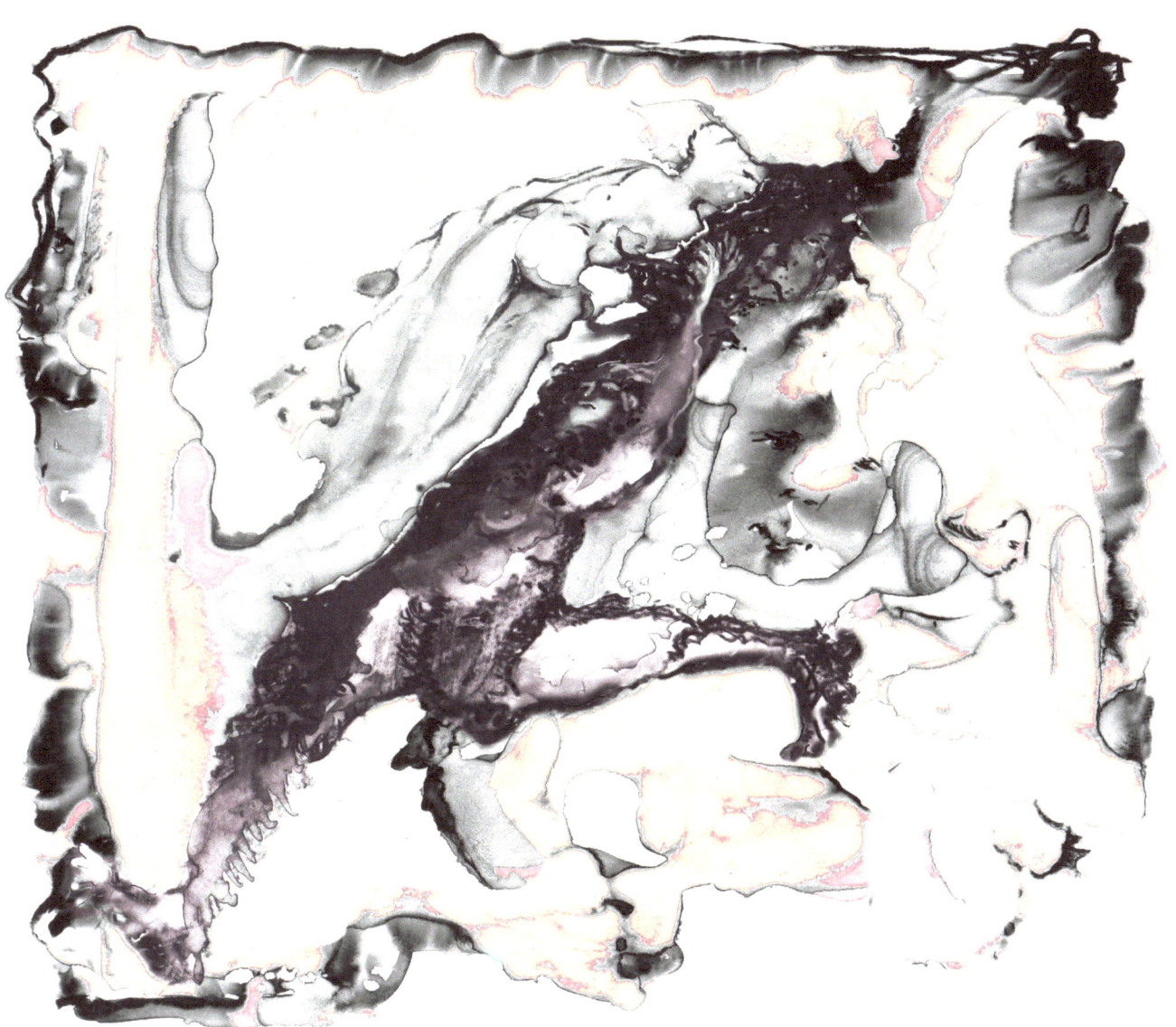

Woman Fleeing

The Tao teaches us balance, holding
inner and outer, right and wrong, all
dichotomies, together in Oneness.

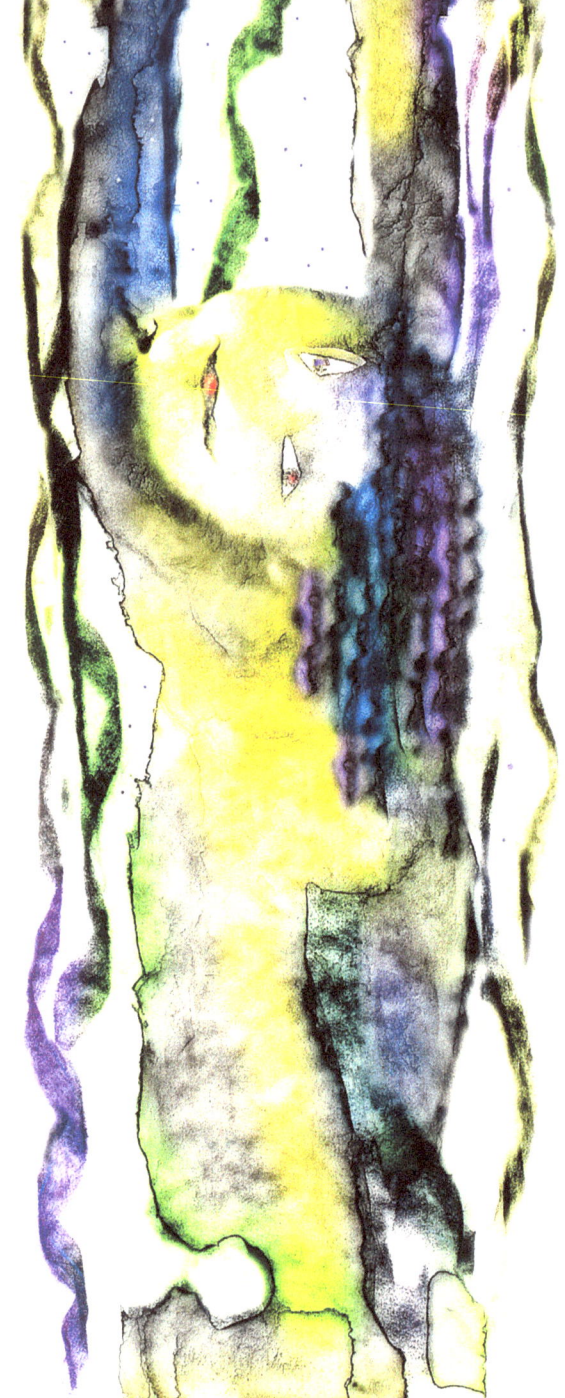

Salome

"...recognize this world
is a cosmic dance,
the dance of form,
no more and no less."
ECKHART TOLLE
Stillness Speaks, 2003

A Brief Bio

Since the early 1950's I have been continually involved with visual arts: BA degree from Pennsylvania State University, fine arts major; MA degree from Columbia University, Teachers' College, fine arts major; Parsons School of Design, advertising curriculum: Brooklyn Museum of Art, oil painting with Reuben Tam; extensive professonal experience in textile design, packaging design graphics, corporate identitiy programs, and finally teaching 22 years at the Fashion Institute of Technology (State Univeristy of New York) in New York City.

At FIT I taught textile (graphic) design from January 1975 to October 1997 in the Textile/Surface Design Department. Classes covered products from Home Furnishings to Apparel Fabric Prints; color fundamentals for beginning students; writing syllabi for advanced design classes in the upper division curriculum. The focus was on the current marketplace needs as well as the print technology necessary for industry. While at FIT, in collaboration with a fellow faculty member, I wrote the department textbook: *Textile Print Design*, Fairchild Publications, 1987.

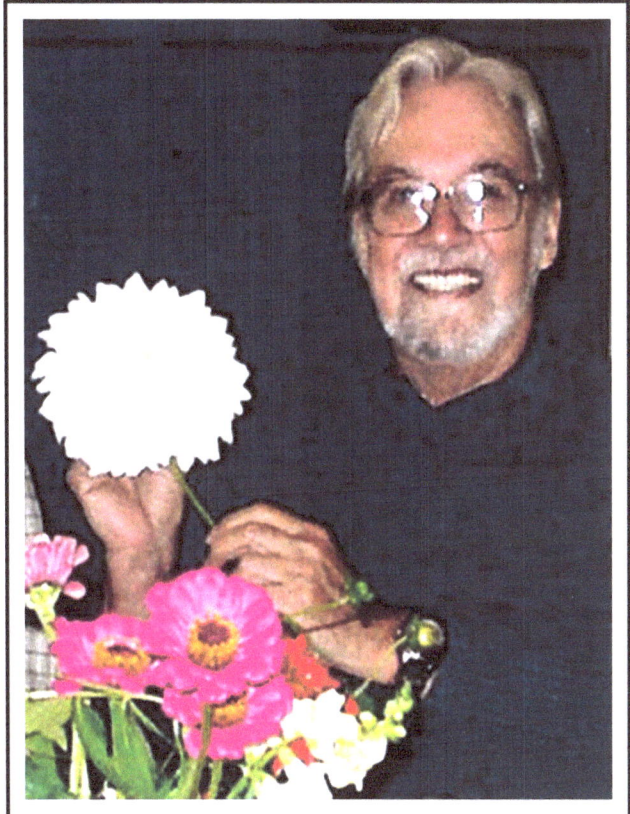

Upon retiring from teaching I have developed my own unique approach to art and the creative processes. At the core of this work are drawing meditations. Inspired by Carl Jung, (the psychology of the mind), Anton Erhnesweig (the education of vision), Leonardo da Vinci (on creativity), and by artists such as Hieronymous Bosch, William Blake, Odilon Redon, Max Ernst to name a few, I continue to 'draw forth' MINDWORKS images from the unconscious mind.

Richard Fisher